CONSTITUTIONAL AND ADMINISTRATIVE LAW

UPDATING SUPPLEMENT

The contents of this Supplement, prepared by Anthony Bradley and Keith Ewing, deal with important developments that have occurred since the text of the 15th edition was finalised in the summer of 2010 and before 31 May 2013. For ease of use, the developments detailed in these notes are cross-referenced to the relevant chapters and page numbers of the 15th edition.

PEARSON

At Pearson, we take learning personally. Our courses and resources are available as books, online and via multi-lingual packages, helping people learn whatever, wherever and however they choose.

We work with leading authors to develop the strongest learning experiences, bringing cutting-edge thinking and best learning practice to a global market. We craft our print and digital resources to do more to help learners not only understand their content, but to see it in action and apply what they learn, whether studying or at work.

Pearson is the world's leading learning company. Our portfolio includes Penguin, Dorling Kindersley, the Financial Times and our educational business, Pearson International. We are also a leading provider of electronic learning programmes and of test development, processing and scoring services to educational institutions, corporations and professional bodies around the world.

Every day our work helps learning flourish, and wherever learning flourishes, so do people.

To learn more please visit us at: www.pearson.com/uk

CONSTITUTIONAL AND ADMINISTRATIVE LAW

FIFTEENTH EDITION

UPDATING SUPPLEMENT

A W Bradley MA, LLM, LLD, QC (Hon)
Emeritus Professor of Constitutional Law,
University of Edinburgh;
Barrister, of the Inner Temple;
Institute of European and Comparative Law,
University of Oxford

K D Ewing LLB, PhD
Professor of Public Law,
King's College, London

PEARSON

Harlow, England • London • New York • Boston • San Francisco • Toronto • Sydney
Auckland • Singapore • Hong Kong • Tokyo • Seoul • Taipei • New Delhi
Cape Town • São Paulo • Mexico City • Madrid • Amsterdam • Munich • Paris • Milan

Pearson Education Limited
Edinburgh Gate
Harlow CM20 2JE
United Kingdom
Tel: +44 (0)1279 623623
Web: www.pearson.com/uk

First published 2013 (print)

ISBN: 978-1-447-92381-7 (print)
       978-1-292-00345-0 (eText)

British Library Cataloguing-in-Publication Data
A catalogue record for the print edition is available from the British Library

Library of Congress Cataloging-in-Publication Data
Bradley, A. W. (Anthony Wilfred)
    Constitutional and administrative law / A.W. Bradley, K.D. Ewing. -- 15th ed.
    p. cm
    Includes bibliographical references and index.
    ISBN 978-1-447-92381-7
    1. Constitutional law -- Great Britain. 2 Administrative law -- Great Britain. I. Title.
KD3930.W3 2010
342.41--dc22
                                                                              2010023415

10 9 8 7 6 5 4 3 2 1
16 15 14 13

Print edition typeset in 9.5/11.5pt Sabon by 35
Print edition printed and bound in the United Kingdom by Henry Ling, Dorcherter, Dorset

NOTE THAT ANY PAGE CROSS REFERENCES REFER TO THE PRINT EDITION

Contents

Chapter 29 ADMINISTRATIVE JUSTICE

Chapter 30 JUDICIAL REVIEW OF ADMINISTRATIVE ACTION I

Chapter 31 JUDICIAL REVIEW OF ADMINISTRATIVE ACTION II

Chapter 32 LIABILITY OF PUBLIC AUTHORITIES AND THE CROWN

Table of Cases

Table of Statutes

BRADLEY AND EWING
15TH EDITION SUPPLEMENT
INTRODUCTION

This short supplement is designed to update the text of our book, *Constitutional and Administrative Law* (15th ed., 2011). We must emphasise that in the space available it has not been possible to take in all the changes that have taken place since the general election of 2010, which was the cut-off point for the last edition. As a bridge between the 15th and 16th editions (now in preparation), it may nevertheless be valuable to provide an account of some major developments that have taken place in the first three years of the planned five-year tenure of the Coalition government. A coalition government is itself a highly unusual event in British politics, but one to which our constitutional arrangements have adapted with relative ease, even if the politics have at times been turbulent.

The modern programme of constitutional reform started in earnest with the Blair government elected in 1997, leading within a few years to devolution, the Human Rights Act 1998 and the House of Lords Act 1999. Other major changes were to follow, the most notable of which was the Constitutional Reform Act 2005. But the political parties in the present government have their own priorities for constitutional change, whether it be a rebalancing of the United Kingdom's relationship with Europe (in the case of the Conservative party), or electoral reform and finishing the business on House of Lords reform (in the case of the Liberal Democrats). It is also the case that the constitutional reforms of the late 1990s – notably devolution and human rights – have for various reasons had to be revisited.

In addressing these and other issues in this supplement, we also consider some leading decisions of the courts, which continue to enrich our jurisprudence and enlighten understanding of our constitutional arrangements. But it is not possible to address every theme, and some matters have been held over to the 16th edition. These include the proposals by Lord Justice Leveson (published on 29 November 2012) for the better regulation of the press, in the light of the misbehaviour of some of its practitioners and the ineffectiveness of existing forms of regulation. At the time of writing, this is very much a work in progress, and it is uncertain whether and to what extent the Leveson recommendations will be implemented, or whether alternative arrangements will be put in place.

References in the pages that follow to 'the text' are references to *Constitutional and Administrative Law*, 15th edition.

Anthony Bradley
Keith Ewing
May 2013

Chapter 3

THE STRUCTURE OF THE UNITED KINGDOM

Pages 42-44
Devolution to Scotland

The report of the Calman Commission on Scottish devolution, *Serving Scotland Better: Scotland and the United Kingdom in the 21st Century* (text, page 44) made many recommendations for extending the powers devolved to the Scottish Parliament and Ministers by the Scotland Act 1998. The Coalition government in London, formed after the UK general election in May 2010, agreed to implement the Calman recommendations. In the election for the Scottish Parliament in 2011, the Scottish National Party (which had earlier opposed the creation of the Calman Commission) for the first time secured an absolute majority of seats in the Parliament. Negotiations between Scottish Ministers and London eventually led to the Scotland Act 2012 being enacted at Westminster, with the consent of the Scottish Parliament (given on 18 April 2012, in so far as it was needed under the 'Sewel convention' – text, page 43).

The Act of 2012 made many amendments to the Scotland Act 1998. Part 1 transferred from the Secretary of State for Scotland to Scottish Ministers power to make subordinate legislation governing the conduct of elections, subject to consultation with the Electoral Commission. Part 2 of the Act included (in s 12) a change in the name of the Scottish administration, from Scottish Executive to Scottish Government. Section 14 introduced a twelve-month time-limit (as in the Human Rights Act 1998, s 7(5)) for actions against Scottish Ministers that are based on breaches of Convention rights, and for that reason are outside the devolved competence of the Ministers.[1] Section 15 authorised a court to limit or exclude the retrospective effect of court decisions where non-legislative acts are held to be outside devolved competence. Part 3 of the Act is notable for expanding the powers of the Scottish Parliament to impose income tax on those who are 'Scottish taxpayers' (text, page 43); it also devolved to Scotland the power to legislate on stamp duty for property transactions, and landfill charges. Part 4 is mainly concerned with changes in the process to be followed when criminal proceedings raise issues as to the compatibility of Scottish procedure with EU law or the European Convention on Human Rights.

---

[1] In *Somerville v Scottish Ministers* [2007] UKHL 44, [2007] 1 WLR 2734, the House of Lords by 3-2 had held that a claim for damages based on breach of the claimant's Convention rights could be brought either under the Human Rights Act 1998, in which case the twelve-month time limit applied, or under the Scotland Act 1998, which imposed no time-limit. The main effect of this decision had already been reversed by the Scottish Parliament, using emergency procedure (see the Convention Rights Proceedings (Amendment) (Scotland) Act 2009).

This last group of changes largely arose from the decision of the UK Supreme Court in *Cadder* v *Her Majesty's Advocate*,[2] when the seven-judge court held that the power of the police to question suspects for up to six hours under the Criminal Procedure (Scotland) Act 1995, s 14, without a lawyer being present, was incompatible with the right to a fair trial guaranteed by Article 6 ECHR. The Scottish Parliament had responded quickly to *Cadder* by enacting the Criminal Procedure (Legal Assistance, Detention and Appeals) (Scotland) Act 2010, which accepted the central decision in *Cadder,* but made other changes in the law on police questioning. The Supreme Court's decision in *Cadder* was unpopular with those in Scotland, including SNP ministers, who felt that judicial decisions under the Scotland Act and the Human Rights Act went too far in enabling questions of Scottish criminal law to be decided in London by the Supreme Court: previously, all such questions had been decided finally by the High Court of Justiciary in Edinburgh.

After the success of the SNP in the 2011 elections, Scottish Ministers began to prepare for the holding of a referendum on whether devolution should give way to independence for Scotland. Early in 2012, the governments in London and Edinburgh each issued a consultation paper on this far-reaching question[3] that involved the making of unprecedented political calculations. The Scotland Act 1998 had reserved from devolution the power to legislate on certain 'aspects of the constitution', including 'the Union of the Kingdoms of Scotland and England'.[4] Despite the view of Scottish Ministers that this did not exclude the holding of an advisory referendum, an alternative legal view was that an independence referendum would be lawful only if authorised by a UK Act or if an Order in Council were to modify the Scotland Act list of reserved matters.[5] In October 2012, the two governments reached an agreement in Edinburgh[6] that was intended to create a 'clear legal basis' for a referendum on independence, that would command confidence in the outcome and provide a 'fair and decisive expression' of the Scottish electorate's opinion. The main features of the Edinburgh agreement were: (a) an Order in Council to be made under the Scotland Act 1998, s 30(2) to authorise the Scottish Parliament to legislate on an independence referendum; (b) the referendum to be held not later than 31 December 2014, and not on the date of any other poll held under the Scotland Act; (c) the ballot paper to contain only one question, with voters having to choose between two responses; and (d) the referendum to

---

[2] [2010] UKSC 43, [2010] 1 WLR 2601. This outcome was based on the decision of the Strasbourg Court in *Salduz* v *Turkey* (2008) 49 EHRR 421, which had previously been considered but not followed by seven Scottish High Court judges in *Her Majesty's Advocate* v *McLean* 2009 HCJAC 97, 2010 SLT 73.

[3] See *Scotland's Constitutional Future* (Cm 8203, 2012) and Scottish Ministers, *Your Scotland, Your Referendum* (January 2012).

[4] Scotland Act 1998, s 30 and Sch 5, para 1 (b).

[5] See House of Lords Constitution Committee, 24th report (HL paper 263, 2010–12) and 7th report (HL paper 62, 2012–13).

[6] Agreement between the UK Government and the Scottish Government on a referendum on independence for Scotland, 15 October 2012.

be conducted in principle in accordance with the Political Parties, Elections and Referendums Act 2000 (text, pages 156, 165).[7] The date for the poll was later set at 18 September 2014, and the proposed question on the ballot paper will be 'Should Scotland be an independent country?' This legislation is limited to the holding of the referendum and does not address the further measures that might follow a majority vote in favour of independence.

From the outset of devolution, the Scottish Parliament's power to make laws for Scotland (text, pages 42–44) has been subject to the limits set out in the Scotland Act 1998. The Act provided procedures for enabling the courts to decide disputes over the extent of the limits, but it did not settle what the approach of the courts should be in determining those limits, and it did not deal with the question of whether there might be limits derived not from the 1998 Act but from the common law on judicial review. In *AXA General Insurance, Ltd, Petitioners*,[8] these matters came before the UK Supreme Court. The AXA litigation was occasioned by the decision of the House of Lords in *Rothwell* v *Chemical Insulating Co Ltd*[9] which had held (reversing earlier decisions) that the physical condition known as asymp-tomatic pleural plaques (often caused by inhaling asbestos fibres) was not in itself an injury that gave rise to a claim in tort. This decision would have deprived many persons exposed to asbestos of any chance of compensation. In England and Wales, the UK government created a non-statutory compensation fund, but in Scotland the Damages (Asbestos-related conditions) (Scotland) Act 2009 was passed to declare that such pleural plaques were a personal injury that constituted actionable harm. The companies that had insured employers against their liability for personal injuries to employees challenged the validity of the Act, claiming that its effect was to deprive them retrospectively of their possessions under Article 1, First Protocol to the ECHR (text, page 400) and in any event that, as a matter of common law, the Act was irrational, unreasonable or arbitrary (text, pages 679–682). The insurance companies' claims failed both in the Scottish courts, and also in the Supreme Court, where the leading judgments were given by the Scottish justices, Lords Hope and Reed. They held that the Act of 2009 did not lack a reasonable foundation and was not manifestly unreasonable or disproportionate. The promotion of social justice was a legitimate purpose within European Convention case-law. As for judicial review at common law, the supervisory jurisdiction of the courts that exists under

---

[7] See the Scotland Act 1998 (Modification of Schedule 5) Order 2013, SI 2013 No 242. Two Bills to govern the holding of the referendum were introduced in the Scottish Parliament during March 2013: the Scottish Independence Referendum (Franchise) Bill, and the Scottish Independence Referendum Bill.

[8] [2011] UKSC 46, 2011 SLT 1061. On an earlier challenge to the validity of a Scottish Act that increased the power of the sheriff in a criminal case to imprison someone convicted of driving without a licence, the Supreme Court by 3-2 upheld the Act as being primarily concerned with criminal procedure, rather than road traffic law (a matter reserved to the UK Parliament): *Martin and Miller* v *Lord Advocate* [2010] UKSC 10, 2010 SLT 412.

[9] [2007] UKHL 39, [2008] 1 AC 281.

Scots law (text, page 725) was not expressly excluded by the Scotland Act 1998 and might in extreme cases be exercised, but its application to the Scottish Parliament (a democratically elected legislature) raised very different considerations from its application to an executive body in Scotland. Lord Hope and Lord Reed separately discussed the constitutional principles that might be relevant to such review. They were aware of comments on the sovereignty of the UK Parliament in *R (Jackson)* v *Attorney General* (text, pages 65–66), and were reluctant to rule out any possibility of judicial review of a Scottish Act, but they gave little indication of how this theoretical possibility might be exercised. Two brief comments may be made:[10] (a) for the judges to have found that the Scottish Parliament did not have power to enact this legislation would have caused a severe blow to the Parliament's authority, and would have provoked criticism of the legitimacy of such a ruling; and (b) given that Scottish Acts must in any event comply with EU law and the ECHR, it will indeed be a rare event for the courts to consider creating a separate heading of review at common law. Finally, *AXA General Insurance* is notable for making an important change in the Scottish law of judicial review regarding standing to sue (text, pages 724–726, and comment on Chapter 31 below).

Pages 44-46
Devolution to Wales

In 2011, giving effect to one aspect of the Coalition agreement in May 2010, and with the support of the Welsh Government and the Welsh political parties, the Secretary of State for Wales established an independent, cross-party commission (known as the Silk Commission, after its chairman) (i) to review the case for devolving fiscal powers to the National Assembly for Wales and for improving the Assembly's financial accountability, and (ii) to consider the need for other changes in the arrangements in place after the Government of Wales Act 2006. In 2012, the Commission reported on part (i) of its remit.[11] The report, in some ways resembling recommendations by the Calman Commission for Scotland, criticised the current scheme of funding the Welsh administration by a block grant from London, as not affording due accountability to the Welsh people; it recommended the conferring of a limited power to impose income tax on Welsh taxpayers, and devolution of business rates and land-related taxes, including stamp duty. Since the devolving of income tax would represent a 'fundamental shift' in powers from London to Cardiff, the Commission recommended that this should be preceded by a referendum of the Welsh people.

---

[10] Cf C Himsworth, [2012] PL 205, 210.
[11] *Empowerment and Responsibility: Financial Powers to Strengthen Wales*, November 2012.

In 2012, the Supreme Court was asked to consider whether the Local Government (Wales) Bill 2012, passed by the Welsh Assembly as an exercise of legislative power made possible by the Government of Wales Act 2006 (text, page 45), was indeed within the legislative competence of the Assembly.[12] The aim of the Bill was to simplify procedures for making local authority byelaws in Wales and it sought to dispense with the need for certain byelaws to be confirmed by Welsh Ministers or the Secretary of State for Wales. On a key point of statutory interpretation, the Supreme Court held that an earlier provision that certain additional functions of the Welsh Assembly might be exercisable by it 'concurrently with the Secretary of State' meant that either the Welsh Assembly or the Secretary of State could exercise those functions, and they did not have to be exercised jointly. This interpretation enabled the court to uphold the validity of the Bill that had been referred to it.

Pages 47-48
The 'West Lothian question'

In 2013, an independent commission, chaired by Sir William McKay, a former Clerk to the House of Commons, issued a report that addressed what has become known as the 'West Lothian question', or the 'English question' (text, page 48).[13] The commission's remit was to examine the consequences of devolution for the House of Commons, in particular to examine how that House might best deal with legislation that affected only England (or England and Wales) in the light of the legislative powers devolved to Scotland, Northern Ireland and Wales. The commission formulated the principle that decisions at the UK level on proposals that had a separate effect on England (or England and Wales) should normally be taken only with the consent of a majority of MPs for England (or for England and Wales, as the case might be). Such a principle should be adopted by resolution of the House of Commons. While this would require separate consideration to be given by the UK government to the interests of England (or England and Wales), the right of the whole House of Commons to decide on such legislation should remain. The McKay report also examined the difficult practical question of how best within the proceedings of the Commons a way could be found of giving effect to this principle. In outlining various proposals for establishing committees limited to MPs from England (or England and Wales), it rejected the idea that MPs elected from areas of the United Kingdom that were not directly affected by a Bill should be barred from voting on it. The McKay Commission's remit did not extend to the House of Lords.

---

[12] *Attorney General's Reference, Re Local Government Byelaws (Wales) Bill 2012* [2012] UKSC 53, [2013] 1 All ER 1013.

[13] Report of the Independent Commission, *The Consequences of Devolution for the House of Commons* (May 2013).

Chapter 4

PARLIAMENTARY SUPREMACY

Pages 69-71
British membership of the European Union (and text, pages 126-129)

The effect of EU membership on the supremacy of Parliament arose in the unusual case of *R v Budimir*.[14] The contents of the Video Recording Act 1984 (text, pages 504, 510) had not been notified in advance to the European Commission as required by the Technical Standards Directive 83/189/EEC. Under European law, the omission made the Act unenforceable in United Kingdom courts, but this was discovered by the British government only in 2009, by which time many convictions under the 1984 Act had occurred. The government at once notified Brussels of the law and caused Parliament rapidly to enact the Video Recordings Act 2010 in the same terms as in 1984. In *R v Budimir*, a company that had been convicted and fined for breach of the 1984 Act claimed that the conviction should be quashed because of the non-notification; another company sought leave to appeal out of time against conviction. The Court of Appeal held that breach of the Directive may have rendered the 1984 Act unenforceable, but did not render the Act a nullity. In the court's view, the conduct of the companies was criminal under the 1984 Act and remained so under the 2010 Act. No substantial injustice would be done if the court did not reopen the convictions; national rules on criminal appeals did not infringe the principle of effectiveness in EU law. Moreover, Article 7 ECHR (prohibition of retrospective laws) did not require that the convictions be reopened. It is remarkable both that on this matter the ordinary process of legislation at Westminster was not sufficient for Parliament to enact an enforceable law, and also that the court could hold that the legislative authority of Parliament had not lost all its effectiveness.

In its *Programme for Government*, adopted in May 2010 (see below, pages 8–10), the Coalition government undertook to 'examine the case for a United Kingdom Sovereignty Bill to make it clear that the ultimate authority remains with Parliament'. This examination resulted in the European Union Act 2011. Part 1 of the Act contains extensive provisions that restrict the authority of the UK government to ratify changes in the European treaties and to approve other decisions relating to EU law. These provisions fall into two broad categories: (a) those that require the government to obtain the express approval of *Parliament* to the changes, that approval to be given by an Act of Parliament or, in specified cases, by a government motion adopted by each House; and (b) those that go further by requiring the Act of Parliament that gives such approval to authorise a *referendum*

---

[14] [2010] EWCA Crim 1486, [2011] 3 All ER 206.

6

of the UK electorate, at which the majority of those voting favour the proposed change.

The Act serves broad political purposes in guarding against any new transfer of powers from London to Brussels and in ensuring that reforms in the EU system will not be adopted by the government without approval from Parliament. The Constitution Committee of the House of Lords welcomed what it termed this 're-balancing of domestic constitutional arrangements in favour of Parliament'.[15] However, the Committee was very critical of the requirement of a national referendum on the detailed matters listed in the Act, drawing attention to the 'complex and highly technical nature of the referendum lock provisions', many of which did not raise the 'fundamental constitutional issues on which a UK-wide referendum may be judged to be appropriate'.[16] Moreover, the 2011 Act includes nothing that seeks to 'entrench' the requirement of a referendum against modification or repeal by a later Parliament. On the orthodox view of Parliament's legislative supremacy, even if such a clause had been included, the attempt could not be effective. Parliament may indeed impose limitations on the future power of the *government* to ratify treaties, and these limitations will remain in force until repealed by a later Act. It is quite a different matter for today's Parliament to stipulate how a future *Parliament* should legislate. While any attempt to depart from the EU Act 2011 might give rise to political difficulties, depending on the circumstances, a future Parliament could always legislate on EU affairs in a manner that expressly or by implication dispensed with the need for a referendum.

Section 18 of the 2011 Act contains what has sometimes been described inaccurately as 'the sovereignty clause'. Entitled 'Status of EU law dependent on continuing statutory basis', s 18 states:

> Directly applicable or directly effective EU law (that is, the rights, powers, liabilities, obligations, restrictions, remedies and procedures referred to in section 2(1) of the European Communities Act 1972) falls to be recognised and available in law in the United Kingdom only by virtue of that Act or where it is required to be recognised and available in law by virtue of any other Act.

Expert evidence to the Commons European Scrutiny Committee[17] confirmed that this was a declaration of the long-established rule (reflecting the common law tradition of 'dualism') that treaties entered into by the government have legal effect within the United Kingdom only where Parliament has authorised this (see Chapter 15B). Was there any need for this new declaratory statement? Enactment of the section may have to an extent placated some Euro-sceptics in Parliament, although they would have preferred express protection for the sovereignty of Parliament and/or national sovereignty. The government's justification for s 18 was

---

[15] Constitution Committee, 13th report (HL Paper 121, 2010–12), *European Union Bill*.
[16] Ibid, para 38.
[17] See *The EU Bill and Parliamentary Sovereignty*, 10th report of the European Scrutiny Committee (HC 633, 2010–11), vols 1 and 2.

that it provides 'clear authority which can be relied upon to counter arguments that EU law constitutes a new higher autonomous legal order derived from the EU treaties or international law and principles which has become an integral part of the UK's legal system independent of statute'.[18] This refers to an argument by counsel that was rejected by the court in *Thoburn* v *Sunderland Council*.[19] Those who wish to defend national sovereignty against the 'incoming tide' of EU law may see s 18 as forestalling any argument that the Westminster Parliament has no power to repeal the European Communities Act 1972 (even if such argument would have little chance of success). Being expressly limited to the context of EU law, s 18 has no bearing on the general question of whether there are 'constitutional statutes' in the United Kingdom that are not subject to implied repeal.[20]

Chapter 7

RESPONSIBLE AND ACCOUNTABLE GOVERNMENT

The formation of the Coalition government after the general election in May 2010 was for the United Kingdom an unusual political event, which might have been thought to require a wholesale re-working of the principles on which responsible government is based, for example a completely new *Ministerial Code* (see text, pages 114, 271–272). In fact, as one study of the Coalition government has commented, the Coalition 'spawned a determination to review cabinet government, and to use Cabinet and its Committees as the prime machinery for negotiation between the coalition partners, and for resolving coalition disputes'.[21] The key document on which the Coalition government has operated is the lengthy and detailed *Programme for Government*, containing the substantive issues on which the two parties reached agreement, or in some instances agreed to differ. This was followed by a procedural agreement, entitled *Coalition Agreement for Stability and Reform*.[22] In setting out the agreed methods in Whitehall and at Westminster for ensuring parliamentary support for the Coalition government, this latter document stated: 'There is no constitutional difference between a Coalition Government and a single party Government, but working practices need to adapt to reflect the fact that the UK has

---

[18] European Union Act 2011, Explanatory Note on s 18.

[19] [2002] EWHC 195 (Admin); [2003] QB 151. And text, pages 67, 140–1.

[20] See text pages 59–60, 67, 69, 140–1.

[21] R Hazell and B Yong, *The Politics of Coalition: How the Conservative-Liberal Democrat Government works* (2012), p 51. For a different account, written from a broader political and constitutional perspective, see V Bogdanor, *The Coalition and the Constitution* (2011).

[22] For this document and the *Programme for Government*, see the Cabinet Office web-site. The *Coalition Agreement for Stability and Reform* is also in Hazell and Yong, app 4.

not had a Coalition in modern times'. In a similar vein, the departments were told by the Cabinet Secretary, Sir Gus O'Donnell: 'The role of the Civil Service is to serve the Government of the day. This is of course no different for a coalition government, with majority and minority partners.'[23]

When the Prime Minister, David Cameron, issued a new version of the *Ministerial Code*, the main alteration from the former text was to the general statement of collective responsibility (text, page 105), which as revised in 2010 reads: 'The principle of collective responsibility, *save where it is explicitly set aside*, requires that Ministers should be able to express their views frankly in the expectation that they can argue freely in private while maintaining a united front when decisions have been reached' (italics supplied).[24] The italicised phrase was inserted to give effect to those issues on which the Coalition partners had agreed to maintain their separate views. These included the holding of a national referendum on the parliamentary voting system (in the campaigning for this referendum, the Conservative and Liberal Democrat parties were on opposite sides), the reduction in the size of the House of Commons and the issue of a British Bill of Rights. The fact that the two partners were at odds on such issues was well known, but for parliamentary purposes collective responsibility was maintained. As has been commented, 'The Government displayed exemplary collective cabinet responsibility, with the only lapse being the Prime Minister's outbursts against the Human Rights Act, which appeared at times to undermine his own Government's commission.'[25] But while ministers may have observed their collective duties, this did not always guarantee a speedy passage of legislation through Parliament. 'However faithful the Government's commitment . . . to collective responsibility and to defending the compromises they had agreed, they could not always deliver their supporters in Parliament.'[26]

Other effects of the Coalition on responsible government included a limitation on the powers of the Prime Minister in such matters as the appointment of ministers, since the Coalition agreement set out the agreed division of ministerial positions between the two parties. Moreover, the need for each partner to maintain its own identity as a political party (for instance, by contesting by-elections against each other) inevitably weakened the principle that ministers in the same government must always be seen publicly to be united in their support for agreed policies. The principle of secrecy for discussions within government, between ministers and departments, came under greater pressure than ever (cf text, page 106).

The principle of individual ministerial responsibility (text, pages 108–110) has continued to apply. Two Cabinet ministers (Mr Laws and Dr Fox) resigned over aspects of their private lives and personal interests respectively which made it impossible for them to continue as ministers, and a third Cabinet minister (Mr Huhne)

---

[23] Letter from Sir Gus O'Donnell to permanent secretaries, Hazell and Yong, app 5.
[24] *Ministerial Code* (Cabinet Office, 2010), para 2.1.
[25] Hazell and Yong, p 170.
[26] Ibid.

resigned to defend himself against criminal charges, for which he was later convicted and had to leave the Commons. The difficulties of the Home Office in maintaining an efficient system of immigration control led to the Home Secretary blaming the senior official concerned for a serious lapse in the system, this being disputed by the official in question. In 2013, the Home Secretary disbanded the UK Border Agency and ministers resumed direct control of the immigration and visa service and a new law enforcement command.[27]

Chapter 8

THE UNITED KINGDOM
AND THE EUROPEAN UNION

Page 133
EU Law and British constitutional law

The European Union Act 2011 introduces a number of innovations designed to give more parliamentary and popular control over decisions affecting the European Union. At least so far as the former is concerned, however, this is consistent with Article 12 of the new Treaty on European Union (TEU), which is designed to enhance the role of national parliaments generally in the work of the EU.[28]

Status of EU law

As pointed out above (pages 6–8,), the European Union Act 2011 purports to make two constitutional innovations. These are rooted in political debates about national sovereignty and legal debates about parliamentary sovereignty. At the level of constitutional principle, the Act provides by s 18 that

> Directly applicable or directly effective EU law (that is, the rights, powers, liabilities, obligations, restrictions, remedies and procedures referred to in section 2(1) of the European Communities Act 1972) falls to be recognised and available in law in the United Kingdom only by virtue of that Act or where it is required to be recognised and available in law by virtue of any other Act.

---

[27] These developments were overseen closely by the Commons Home Affairs Select Committee: see for the 2010–2012 session of Parliament, the Committee's 4th Report (HC 587), 9th Report (HC 907), 15th Report (HC 1497) and 21st Report (HC 1722).

[28] See also Protocol 1 (text, page 137).

As already indicated above, it is unclear what this adds to the existing law: to the extent that EU law has direct effect in the United Kingdom and is applicable by the British courts, this is and can be only by virtue of an Act of Parliament.

The Act of Parliament in question is the European Communities Act 1972, which provides that directly effective EU law (such as provisions in the EU treaties) is to have direct effect by virtue of that enactment.[29] The Act of 1972 (introduced by a Conservative government) also provides that a directly effective EU law is to take priority over any inconsistent Act of Parliament,[30] a provision which at least in its operation some commentators see as a direct threat to the sovereignty of Parliament. It is true that the courts have refused to apply an Act of Parliament that was inconsistent with Community law.[31] Nevertheless, as pointed out in Chapter 8 of the text, it is always possible as a matter of formal legality for Parliament to say in a future Act that it is to take priority over any obligation arising under EU law to the contrary. In that situation, constitutional orthodoxy suggests that the duty of the courts would be to follow the Act of Parliament.[32]

Requirement of a referendum

The other provisions of the European Union Act 2011 may well have greater practical effect, and are both more controversial and more novel. Thus, any further amendment to the EU treaties or any further extension of the powers of the EU institutions at the expense of national sovereignty will first need to be approved by an Act of Parliament **and** by a referendum.[33] This is not simply an advisory referendum, but a requirement that the government shall not ratify a treaty until the referendum has been held and the referendum result is in favour of ratification. This in effect gives to the electorate the legal right of political veto over the actions of the government and the wishes of Parliament, and may be seen as a vindication of popular sovereignty at the expense of parliamentary sovereignty. Parliament may approve the treaty, but the electorate may not, in which case the will of Parliament must give way to the will of the people.

For these purposes, the European Union Act 2011 distinguishes between (i) new treaties amending the EU Treaties, and (ii) revisions to the existing treaties by invoking powers in the Treaty of European Union (TEU). Section 2 of the 2011 Act provides that no treaty amending the TEU or the Treaty on the Functioning of the European Union (TFEU) is to be ratified unless the treaty is (i) laid before Parliament, (ii) approved in an Act of Parliament, **and** (iii) either the 'referendum condition' or the 'exemption condition' is met. The 'referendum condition' is that

---

[29] European Communities Act 1972, s 2.
[30] Ibid.
[31] R v *Secretary of State for Transport, ex p Factortame (No 2)* [1991] 1 AC 603.
[32] For a fuller discussion, see text, Ch 8D.
[33] European Union Act 2011, s 2.

any Act providing for the approval of a treaty should not come into force **until** a referendum on the treaty has been held, in which a majority of those voting do so in favour of ratification. The 'exemption condition' is that the Act dispensing with the need for an amendment states that the treaty amendment does not fall within the European Union Act 2011, s 4.[34]

By virtue of the European Union Act 2011, s 3, a similar arrangement applies in relation to the less formal revision procedure for making amendments to the TFEU. This procedure is to be found in the TEU, Article 48(6), and requires the unanimous approval of Member States. In the case of the United Kingdom, that approval can now be given only if the procedure referred to in the previous paragraph has been followed, with the qualification that neither the 'referendum condition' nor the 'exemption condition' apply if the Act in question states that the 'significance condition' applies. This means that the decision falls within two of the 13 items listed in s 4 of the 2011 Act above,[35] but the effect in relation to the United Kingdom is not significant. It appears to be accepted that a decision as to which of these conditions applies is one that is subject to judicial review.[36]

This is a very important change, which significantly affects the government's power, and has already been raised as an issue in the context of the 'Eurozone' crisis. The 17 Member States of the Eurozone agreed to set up the European Stability Mechanism to secure economic stability in their countries.[37] This required an amendment to the TFEU under the simplified revision procedure referred to above. The question was whether under the 2011 Act a referendum was necessary in the United Kingdom before the decision was confirmed. This could give rise to great difficulty, especially as the UK would not be bound by the treaty revision (not being a member of the Eurozone), though possibly affected by it. Although UK confirmation of the decision required the approval of Parliament in legislation (by virtue of the 2011 Act), nevertheless it did not require a referendum, it being stated that the referendum condition had not been met (s 1(3)).[38]

This aspect of the European Union Act 2011 is nevertheless extremely significant. If s 18 (referred to above) could be said to be little more than tokenism, the

---

[34] This provides a list of 13 items to which in effect the referendum obligation applies.

[35] Specifically, 'the conferring on an EU institution or body of power to impose a requirement or obligation on the United Kingdom, or the removal of any limitation on any such power of an EU institution or body'; and 'the conferring on an EU institution or body of new or extended power to impose sanctions on the United Kingdom' (s 4(1)(i),(j)).

[36] HL Debs, 23 May 2012 (Lord Howell, Foreign Office Minister of State).

[37] The European Council decision of 25 March 2011 amended TFEU, Art 136 with regard to a stability mechanism for Member States whose currency is the euro (2011/199/EU).

[38] European Union (Approval of Treaty Amendment Decision) Act 2012. The government – which supported the new treaty – could breathe a sigh of relief. See the statement by David Lidington MP, Minister of State at the Foreign and Commonwealth Office, on the Foreign Office Blog, 13 October 2011: http://blogs.fco.gov.uk/davidlidington/2011/10/13/first-use-of-the-european-union-act-2011. See also as not requiring a referendum, the European Union (Croatian Accession and Irish Protocol) Act 2013 (dealing in part with the treaty for the accession of Croatia to the EU, but exempt from the referendum requirement because it 'does not fall within section 4 of the European Union Act 2011' (s 1(3)).

same could not be said of the provisions requiring a referendum. In terms of constitutional law and of implications for the Westminster system, this is probably the most radical of all the Coalition's constitutional initiatives. When the Blair government used the referendum in the context of devolution to Scotland and Wales, it asked the people if they wanted devolution **before** presenting the substantive legislation to Parliament: there was no question of the settled wishes of Parliament being subverted by a referendum. Here we have the possibility for the first time on a national question of great importance of the wishes of Parliament being usurped by the decision of the people.[39]

Parliamentary approval

The requirement for both parliamentary approval by legislation and the need for a referendum does not apply only to treaty amendments (s 2) or treaty revisions (s 3). By virtue of the European Union Act 2011, s 6, it applies also to a wide range of decisions that may be taken by the EU institutions under both the TEU and the TFEU (including any decision to make the euro the currency of the UK), in what is calculated to ensure that these decisions are never likely to be made, at least for the foreseeable future.[40] In addition, s 7 provides for a wide range of decisions that do not need the approval of a referendum but which do need parliamentary approval before they are confirmed by ministers. There are four categories of decision under the TFEU that must be approved by Act of Parliament before they are confirmed, and another six categories of draft decisions under the TEU and the TFEU that must not be supported by ministers unless approved again by Act of Parliament.

The standard procedure is thus that ministers are constrained in many areas from supporting EU initiatives without the authority of an Act of Parliament. The procedure is adapted slightly in the case of decisions taken under TEU, Article 352, which gives a general power by unanimity to take steps to secure one of the objectives of the EU for which no express power is otherwise to be found in the treaties. Before a UK minister supports such a decision, he or she must have parliamentary approval, secured either by an Act of Parliament, or by a resolution passed by both Houses, though the resolution procedure may be adopted only if in the opinion of the minister the measure to which the resolution relates is required as a matter of urgency (s 8).[41] In some cases the need for parliamentary approval in either form may be dispensed with if a minister lays before Parliament a statement specifying a draft decision, and stating that in his or her opinion, the decision relates only to one or more purposes referred to in s 8(6) which are exempt from this procedure.

---

[39] The fate of the Scotland Act 1978, when legislation adopted by Parliament failed to get a sufficient level of support in Scotland to come into force, is an unhappy example of such an approach.

[40] In the event of any such referendum ever taking place, provision is made in s 11 for those entitled to vote (in what would be a national referendum including Gibraltar), while s 13 imposes duties on the Electoral Commission to promote public awareness of the referendum and its subject-matter.

[41] See European Union (Approvals) Act 2013, giving approval for two draft decisions under Art 352.

Chapter 9

COMPOSITION AND MEETING OF PARLIMENT

Page 148
The electoral system

The franchise

The major issue here continues to be the running sore of voting rights for some categories of prisoner (text, page 149), which has not only generated an extraordinary amount of political heat, but also led to an unfortunate conflict between the British government and the European Court of Human Rights (see Chapter 19), which raises fundamental questions about some basic constitutional principles, whatever one may think of the Court's decision (on which reasonable people disagree strongly). In *Hirst* v *United Kingdom (No 2)*,[42] the Court held that the blanket disqualification of prisoners from the franchise violated Article 3 of Protocol 1 (text, page 149). This led in turn to a declaration of incompatibility being made by the Scottish Registration Court in a case involving prisoners.[43]

In 2010 the Strasbourg Court re-affirmed its view on this question in *Greens* v *United Kingdom*,[44] and, being concerned about the delay in implementing *Hirst (No 2)*, imposed a deadline of six months from the date of the former decision, which became final on 11 April 2011. By virtue of this deadline, the government was required to bring forward legislation to amend electoral law to give effect to its obligations under the Convention. The deadline was, however, extended at the request of the British government, which had been permitted to intervene in *Scoppola* v *Italy (No 3)*,[45] another case on prisoners' rights which was before the Court. Under the terms of the extension, the British government was now required to bring forward legislation within six months of the latter decision.

In *Scoppola (No 3)*, the ECtHR re-affirmed the position adopted in *Hirst (No 2)* in a decision adopted on 22 May 2012. In doing so, the Court emphasised that the essence of the problem related to disenfranchisement that affected 'a group of people generally, automatically and indiscriminately, based solely on the fact that they are serving a prison sentence, irrespective of the length of the sentence and irrespective of the nature or gravity of their offence and their individual circumstances'.[46] It was accepted, however, that national governments have a wide

---

[42] [2005] ECHR 681, (2006) 42 EHRR 41.
[43] *Smith* v *Scott* 2007 SLT 137. Subsequent cases in the Scottish, English and Northern Irish courts are discussed in *Greens* v *United Kingdom* [2010] ECHR 1826.
[44] Ibid.
[45] *Scoppola (No. 3)* v *Italy* [2012] ECHR 868.
[46] Ibid, para 96.

discretion as to how to deal with this question, having regard to the types of offences to which disenfranchisement may apply and the procedures to be adopted before it takes effect. But for the British government there was a now a new deadline of 22 November 2012.

Neither Labour nor Coalition governments appear willing to implement the *Hirst (No 2)* decision, despite various forms of encouragement from and concessions made by the Strasbourg Court. Nevertheless, a draft Voting Eligibility (Prisoners) Bill was duly published in 22 November 2012, the Bill setting out three options for change to be considered by a Joint Committee of both Houses, which would take evidence and make recommendations about which if any of these options should be adopted. The first option is to disqualify prisoners sentenced to four years or more in prison from voting; the second is to disqualify prisoners sentenced to more than six months in prison from voting; and the third is to re-enact the existing ban by disqualifying all convicted prisoners from voting.[47]

But although the draft Bill was published on 22 November 2012, it was not until 16 April 2013 that the composition and remit of the Joint Committee were announced,[48] it also being reported that the Joint Committee would take evidence that would examine a wide range of questions before reporting by 31 October 2013.[49] It is unlikely that this matter will be resolved before the election in 2015, and indeed it is significant that, as first published, the Scottish Independence Referendum (Franchise) Bill 2013 provided defiantly that a convicted person will not be permitted to vote in the independence referendum if serving a prison sentence. This is despite the decision not only in *Hirst (No 2)*, but also in *Greens*, which was a case brought by two Scottish prisoners.[50]

The register of electors

In their *Programme for Government*, the Coalition undertook to 'reduce electoral fraud by speeding up the implementation of individual voter registration'.[51] Initiatives to promote this undertaking are to be found in the Electoral Registration and Administration Act 2013, which sets in train the move towards a system of individual rather than household registration of electors (s 1). This, however, is not a wholly uncontroversial initiative, as it is thought by some that individual registration will lead to fewer people being registered, and to fewer people being eligible to vote as a result. The Electoral Registration and Administration Act 2013 does,

---

[47] http://www.official-documents.gov.uk/document/cm84/8499/8499.pdf.

[48] HC Debs, 16 April 2013, col 294 (Leader of the House).

[49] http://www.parliament.uk/business/committees/committees-a-z/joint-select/draft-voting-eligibility-prisoners-bill.

[50] And despite also *Smith* v *Scott*, above, in which a Scottish court declared the existing prisoner disenfranchisement to be incompatible with Convention rights. See also House of Lords Bill 2012, below, where the Deputy Prime Minister was unable to declare that the Bill was fully compatible with Convention rights (Human Rights Act 1998, s 19, see text, page 414) because clause 6 provided for the disqualification of prisoners in the proposed election of members of the House of Lords.

[51] See also Cm 8108, 2011.

nevertheless, retain the annual canvass of households at least for the time being (s 4), with the Act also conferring a power on the appropriate minister to abolish it by order (s 5).

While the duty to carry out the annual canvass continues, the registration officer must invite people in his or her area to apply for registration, 'if (a) the officer is aware of the person's name and address, (b) the person is not registered in the register, and (c) the officer has reason to believe that the person may be entitled to be registered in the register' (s 5). In a notable provision, the Act also provides that a registration officer may follow an 'invitation to register' with a 'requirement to register', after complying with prescribed obligations set out in regulations (s 5(6) (b)). Failure to comply with the requirement to register may lead to the registration officer imposing a civil penalty (s 5(7)), in accordance with a procedure to be set out in regulations, with a right of appeal to the First-tier Tribunal.[52]

It will take some time for the new register to be created, and it is anticipated that it will be used for the first time at the general election in 2015.

Page 152
The distribution of constituencies

The Electoral Registration and Administration Act 2013 amended the Parliamentary Constituencies Act 1986 in the light of a debacle over attempts recently to redistribute boundaries and to reduce the number of seats in the House of Commons to 600. These latter changes had been introduced by the Parliamentary Voting System and Constituencies Act 2011, which radically amended the 1986 Act by increasing the frequency of boundary reviews from periods of between eight and twelve years, to a period of every five years (see text, page 152). In proposing to reduce the number of constituencies to 600, the Parliamentary Voting System and Constituencies Act 2011 also introduced new principles to secure a more equal distribution of constituencies, which was to be completed by October 2013.

The implementation of these measures has, however, been thwarted by the withdrawal of support by Liberal Democrats in the Coalition government. This follows a disagreement between the two governing parties about the implementation of the government's agreed proposals for constitutional reform, the Liberal Democrat resistance to boundary change being seen as retaliation for Conservative resistance to House of Lords reform (see below). The 2015 election will thus be fought on the old boundaries, in what is thought to have been a blow to the Conservative party in particular, it being widely believed that a smaller House of Commons with redistributed boundaries would provide them with more seats in a future Parliament and a better prospect of forming government on their own.

---

[52] Representation of the People Act 1983, s 9E, Sch ZA1, paras 3, 4, and 5.

This disagreement found formal expression in the Electoral Registration and Administration Act 2013, which by s 6 amends the Parliamentary Voting System and Constituencies Act 2011 by providing that there should now be no boundary review until 2018. The process by which the latter provision was introduced was thought to be significant constitutionally, the government splitting on party lines in voting for it (Liberal Democrat) and against it (Conservative). In supporting an amendment to a government Bill, this was 'the first time in this Parliament that ministers in either house have voted against the government'. The Prime Minister's spokesman was also reported as having said that 'the application of collective responsibility has been set aside' for the Electoral Registration and Administration Bill.[53]

The Electoral Registration and Administration Act 2013, s 6, does not repeal the changes introduced by the 2011 Act: it simply postpones their implementation until after the next general election in 2015. If the Conservative Party wins a majority at the election, it is likely that the provisions of the 2011 Act will be fully implemented, and at that stage it will be necessary fully to master the new principles for the redistribution of parliamentary constituencies. If, however, the other parties form the government, either alone or in coalition, it is possible that the relevant provisions of the 2011 Act will be repealed or heavily amended, and that the existing principles for boundary redistribution will be retained with modifications if necessary (see text, page 153).

Page 159
The conduct of elections

As discussed in the text (page 161), the Communications Act 2003 prohibits paid political advertising on television and radio at election and other times (a prohibition introduced with the introduction of commercial television in 1954). The ban was upheld by the European Court of Human Rights in *Animal Defenders International* v *United Kingdom*,[54] where the issue was whether the prohibition could be justified under ECHR Article 10(2), it being accepted by the parties that it was a breach of Article 10(1) and that the breach was 'prescribed by law'. In dividing 9-8 to uphold the ban, the Court revealed this clearly to be a difficult question, albeit that the House of Lords had previously come to a similar conclusion with significantly less division in *R (Animal Defenders International)* v *Secretary of State for Culture, Media and Sport*.[55]

At the heart of the case was the duty of the Strasbourg Court to 'balance, on the one hand, the applicant NGO's right to impart information and ideas of general interest which the public is entitled to receive with, on the other, the authorities'

---

[53] *Guardian*, 29 January 2013. The Deputy Prime Minister was reported earlier as having said that 'conventions mutate and change over time': *Daily Telegraph*, 3 September 2012.
[54] [2013] ECHR 362.
[55] [2008] UKHL 15, [2008] 1 AC 1312.

desire to protect the democratic debate and process from distortion by powerful financial groups with advantageous access to influential media'.[56] In deciding for the government, the majority attached 'considerable weight' to reviews of this question that had been undertaken by the Joint Committee on Human Rights and the Committee on Standards in Public Life.[57] The Court was also influenced by the fact that there was 'no European consensus between Contracting States on how to regulate paid political advertising in broadcasting'.[58]

It is to be noted, however, that the prohibition on political advertising does not apply only to political advertising at election time; indeed there was no suggestion that the applicants wanted to use paid advertising in order to influence the outcome of elections. In rejecting the argument that it would have been possible to protect the integrity of the electoral process by more carefully targeted restrictions that allowed advertising space for social advocacy groups, the majority accepted government arguments that a less restrictive prohibition would give rise to two concerns: a risk of abuse and a risk of arbitrariness.[59] According to the majority, it was 'reasonable to fear that this option [of a more carefully targeted restriction] would give rise to a risk of wealthy bodies with agendas being fronted by social advocacy groups created for that precise purpose'.[60]

Page 163
Supervision of elections

An important reminder of the severe consequences of breaching electoral law is provided by *Watkins* v *Woolas*,[61] where a Labour MP was unseated after the 2010 general election for violating the Representation of the People Act 1983, s 106. The latter provides that before or during an election, it is an offence to make or publish any false statement of fact in relation to a candidate's personal character or conduct, where this is done for the purpose of affecting the return of a candidate at the election.

In the *Watkins* case, Mr Woolas was found by an Election Court to have made three such false statements in relation to his Liberal Democrat rival, whom he had defeated with a majority of only 103 votes. Mr Woolas was said to have made statements that 'were not of a trivial nature; they were a serious personal attack on a candidate by saying he condoned violence by extremists and refused to condemn those who advocated violence'.[62] By virtue of the Representation of the People Act

---

[56] [2013] ECHR 362, para 112.
[57] Ibid, para 116.
[58] Ibid, para 123.
[59] Ibid, para 122.
[60] Ibid.
[61] [2010] EWHC 2702 (QB).
[62] *R (Woolas)* v *Speaker of the House of Commons* [2010] EWHC 3169 (Admin), [2012] QB 1, para 125.

1983, s 159, Mr Woolas's election was held to be void, and as a result of having been found to have committed an illegal practice, he was barred from standing for Parliament. This proved to be a rather pyrrhic victory for Mr Watkins, who lost to the Labour candidate at the subsequent by-election by over 2,000 votes.

Mr Woolas challenged the decision of the Election Court in judicial review proceedings, in a case acknowledged to have raised important constitutional questions about the susceptibility of the Election Court (which consists of High Court judges) to judicial review by the Administrative Court (which consists of other High Court judges).[63] In holding that the latter has the power to review the former in order to prevent any mistakes of law from going unchecked, the Administrative Court overturned one of the findings against Mr Woolas, but not the other two. The case also raised important questions about the relationship between the Representation of the People Act 1983, s 106, and Convention rights, notably Article 10. But according to Thomas LJ:

> Freedom of political debate must allow for the fact that statements are made which attack the political character of a candidate which are false but which are made carelessly. Such statements may also suggest an attack on aspects of his character by implying he is a hypocrite. Again, imposing a criminal penalty on a person who fails to exercise care when making statements in respect of a candidate's political position or character that by implication suggest he is a hypocrite would very significantly curtail the freedom of political debate so essential to a democracy. It could not be justified as representing the intention of Parliament. However, imposing such a penalty where care is not taken in making a statement that goes beyond this and is a statement in relation to the personal character of a candidate can only enhance the standard of political debate and thus strengthen the way in which a democratic legislature is elected.[64]

Page 166
Electoral systems and electoral reform

The Coalition *Programme for Government* addresses two major Liberal Democrat concerns: electoral reform and House of Lords reform. The Liberal Democrats have a particularly strong interest in *electoral reform*. This is because under the first past the post electoral system, they are under-represented in terms of seats in proportion to the number of votes they manage to win. At the general election in 2010, for example, the Liberal Democrats won 23% of the vote but less than 10% of the seats in the House of Commons. However, in proposing electoral reform, the Coalition programme made provision for an electoral system (the alternative vote) that was least likely to deliver a legislature reflecting the national vote. Under the alternative vote, the country would still be divided into single member constituencies.

---

[63] Ibid.
[64] Ibid, para 124.

The only major country to use this system is Australia, where it is said to produce the strongest two party system in the world, with small parties having even greater difficulty in breaking through than under first past the post in the United Kingdom.[65] Nevertheless, the Parliamentary Voting System and Constituencies Act 2011 imposed a duty to bring forward an order to change the existing electoral law if 'more votes are cast in [a] referendum in favour of the answer "Yes" than in favour of the answer "No"'.[66] The referendum was duly held on 5 May 2011, with a large majority in favour of the status quo: 6.1 million voted in favour of change and 13 million against. Most people appeared to be indifferent, with a turnout of only 41.9%, which means that a change to the voting system was supported by only 12% or so of those eligible to vote.

A majority in favour was recorded in only 10 out of 500 voting centres (including Cambridge and Oxford). As a result, it is likely to be a long time before serious attempts are made to change the voting system. Despite its failure to produce a Parliament representative of the nation as a whole; despite its failure to produce MPs who have majority support in their own constituency; and despite the barriers it presents to new parties and small parties from breaking through, first past the post has the virtue of simplicity, even if many now consider it to be old-fashioned. It is not clear if the referendum result would have been different if a different kind of electoral reform had been chosen. But it is to be noted that the electoral system for the Scottish Parliament retains an important first past the post element while managing to deliver a more representative legislature under the 'additional member' system.[67]

Page 177
Membership of the House of Lords

The other major failed initiative relates to *House of Lords reform*, with the Coalition programme committing the parties to 'bring forward proposals for a wholly or mainly elected upper chamber on the basis of proportional representation'. In the meantime, steps would be taken to ensure that the House of Lords was 'reflective of the share of the vote secured by the political parties in the last general election'. On 1 April 2011, the House of Lords consisted of 89 hereditary members, 25 Bishops of the Church of England, and 678 members appointed for life by the Queen on the advice of successive Prime Ministers. This is thought to make the House of Lords one of the largest parliamentary assemblies in the world, and if the government carries out its commitment to make it 'reflective' of the popular

---

[65] See G Orr and K D Ewing, Written Evidence to Political and Constitutional Reform Committee on Parliamentary Voting System and Constituencies Bill, HC 437 (2010–11).
[66] Parliamentary Voting System and Constituencies Act 2011, s 8.
[67] See Scotland Act 1998, s 1.

opinion, its numbers will swell even more. On 1 April 2011, the Conservatives had only 28% of the total and the Liberal Democrats 12%.

The Labour governments from 1997 to 2010 took a number of steps to reform the House of Lords: in 1999, the number of hereditary members was reduced to 92 (text, page 176);[68] and in 2005, the judicial members were removed following the creation of the UK Supreme Court (text, pages 175–176). But more radical reforms in the direction of a wholly or partially elected second chamber proved to be elusive, partly because of a lack of political consensus, and partly because of opposition from the existing House of Lords, without whose consent further reform will be difficult to achieve. At the general election in 2010, all three main political parties made manifesto commitments for further House of Lords reform. After lengthy consultations thereafter, the Deputy Prime Minister introduced a House of Lords Reform Bill in 2012, providing for the phased introduction of a second chamber of 360 directly elected members, plus 90 appointed members, 12 Bishops and an indefinite number of 'ministerial members'.

The elected members would be directly elected by a system of proportional representation for terms of 15 years each, with elections taking place every five years for a third of the seats in the reformed Chamber. It was not proposed under these plans to affect the primacy of the House of Commons, or alter the powers of the House of Lords. Indeed, it was expressly provided that the Parliament Acts 1911–1949 would remain in force, a provision that seemed unnecessary in the light of the lack of any intention to repeal them.[69] The electoral system would be similar to that used for European parliamentary elections, with Great Britain being divided into ten regional constituencies from which members would be elected from party lists (and in Northern Ireland by single transferable vote from a single constituency). But although a well thought-out and elegant solution to an intractable problem, the Bill was lost in the face of strong opposition from Conservative backbenchers.

In fact the Bill was given a second reading in July 2012, though partly as a result of Labour support. But in the face of the opposition from its own benches, the government withdrew the Bill on 3 September 2012, without it having been sent to Committee, ministers being concerned that it would be the subject of protracted proceedings, which would in turn impede the progress of other important parliamentary business. At the same time, the Deputy Prime Minister announced the withdrawal of Liberal Democrat support for the House of Commons membership changes discussed above (the planned reduction in the size of the House to 600, and the redistribution of constituencies to secure constituencies of more equal size). According to Mr Clegg, the two initiatives (Lords and Commons reform respectively) were interconnected. Both parties to the Coalition were thus denied cherished constitutional changes.

---

[68] House of Lords Act 1999; text, Ch 9I.
[69] On the continuing significance of the Parliament Acts, see Lord Pannick [2012] PL 230.

Chapter 11

PRIVILEGES OF PARLIAMENT

MPs and the criminal law

Following the scandal in 2009 regarding MPs' expenses and allowances (text, pages 228–230), several former MPs and members of the House of Lords were prosecuted for having claimed for items such as mortgage payments that had not been made, fictitious travel expenses, and the costs of a 'main residence' that had never been occupied by the member. When the first prosecution was brought against four claimants for having made false statements contrary to the Theft Act 1968, s 17, they asserted (to the indignation of the media) that they were protected by parliamentary privilege, since (i) the claims for expenses were 'proceedings in Parliament' and thus within Article 9 of the Bill of Rights (page 215); and (ii) they came within the internal proceedings of Parliament, over which each House has sole jurisdiction (or 'exclusive cognisance') (page 219).

In *R Chaytor*,[70] a nine-judge Supreme Court unanimously rejected the claim of privilege. Lord Phillips held that the making of claims for allowances and expenses did not form part of, nor was it incidental to, the core or essential business of Parliament. For MPs to be prosecuted for false claims would not inhibit freedom of speech and debate in Parliament. It was for the courts to decide the extent of the protection that Article 9 gave. Where acts of MPs were outside Article 9, they were subject to the criminal law. Lord Phillips cited the dictum of Stephen J, in *Bradlaugh vGossett* (text, page 222), that he knew of 'no authority for the proposition that an *ordinary crime* committed in the . . . Commons would be withdrawn from the ordinary course of criminal justice' (emphasis supplied).[71] The defendants argued that to make false claims might be a contempt of the House, but denied that it was an 'ordinary crime'. The court held that the making of claims for allowances and expenses was not within the 'exclusive jurisdiction' that each House enjoyed over its own procedures.[72] While the House might take disciplinary proceedings for such an act, the courts must deal with charges of criminal conduct where these were outside Article 9.

The Supreme Court's decision on the central issue was inevitable. But the judgments did not resolve all difficulties at the interface between parliamentary privilege and the criminal law, some of which had been exposed by the Damian Green affair (text, page 214).[73] Indeed, the notion of 'ordinary crime' could not have been applied to Mr Green's conduct in his dealings with a civil servant in the Home

---

[70] [2010] UKSC 52, [2011] 1 AC 684.
[71] (1884) 12 QBD 271, 283.
[72] Cf findings by the Parliamentary Commissioner for Standards, which are not subject to judicial review: see page 227, fn 131.
[73] See A W Bradley, [2012] PL 396, 402–4.

Office. As a result of the Green affair, it was insisted by the Speaker that no future police search would take place at Westminster without a search warrant. Yet doubts remain about the exercise of police powers at Westminster and the authority of the Speaker to resist a warrant that a district judge has issued.[74]

The Coalition agreement in May 2010 included a commitment to review the law of parliamentary privilege. Other difficult issues of privilege arose thereafter,[75] and doubts have been expressed over the power of Commons committees to compel members of the public to give evidence.[76] A change in Commons procedure occurred in 2012, when the Committee on Standards and Privileges (text, page 223) was replaced by a Committee on Standards (which in a break from Westminster tradition now includes three members who are not MPs),[77] and a Committee on Privileges. A government Green Paper later declared that it was unnecessary for parliamentary privilege to be codified (as had been recommended in 1999, text, page 213), and made some limited proposals for reform.[78]

Chapter 12

THE CROWN AND THE ROYAL PREROGATIVE

Page 234
The monarchy

Title to the Crown

The Succession to the Crown Act 2013 removes the preference for males over females in determining the succession to the Crown, declaring that 'the gender of a person born after 28 October 2011 does not give that person, or that person's descendants, precedence over any other person (whenever born)' (s 1).

---

[74] Ibid. When a civil servant in New Zealand was sued for defamation in briefing a minister on the reply to a parliamentary question, it was held that (on a test of what was 'necessary' to the working of Parliament) the action was not barred by parliamentary privilege, but that the defence of qualified privilege at common law was available: *Attorney General v Leigh* [2011] NZSC 106; cf *Canada (House of Commons) v Vaid* [2005] SCC 30.

[75] See report of the Neuberger Committee on Super-injunctions (May 2011) and report of the House of Commons Standards and Privileges Committee (HC 628, 2010–12), on the hacking of MPs' mobile phones.

[76] See R Gordon and A Street, *Select Committees and Coercive Powers – Clarity or Confusion* (Constitution Society, 2012).

[77] See 6th report of the Commons Procedure Committee, *Lay membership of the Committee on Standards and Privileges* (2010–12, HC 1605).

[78] *Parliamentary Privilege*, Cm 8318, 2012.

At the time the Act was passed, the Duchess of Cambridge was pregnant and the sex of the unborn child unknown. If, however, the child was female and subsequently had a brother, the female child would now be entitled to succeed to the throne, were she still to be alive on the death of her father, the Duke of Cambridge (assuming that he proceeds to the Throne in due course). This also assumes that the Act is brought fully into force in good time, that is to say before the point of any succession. Until then, as set out in the text (page 234), the rule of primogeniture will continue to apply so that a first born daughter would have to stand aside for a younger brother, although the birth of a boy to the Duchess of Cambridge makes this point of law less urgent.

The other important change introduced by the Succession to the Crown Act 2013 deals with the religious restrictions on succession to the Throne, which by virtue of the Act of Settlement disqualified Roman Catholics and those who married Roman Catholics (text, page 234). Under the 2013 Act, a person is no longer disqualified 'from succeeding to the Crown or from possessing it as a result of marrying a person of the Roman Catholic faith' (s 2(3)). This applies in relation to marriages that took place before the Act came into force, as well as those that take place afterwards. This does not, however, alter the restriction on persons of the Roman Catholic faith from succeeding to the Throne.

Financing the monarchy

The Sovereign Grant Act 2011 introduces a new regime for financing the monarchy. The first of two key features of the replaced regime is that it was 'reign specific', in the sense that provision was made for the monarch at the beginning of his or her reign that would continue until death. The other is that the support consisted of separate allowances, notably the civil list, and the grants in aid for the purposes of royal travel (from the budget of the Department of Transport), and the maintenance of the royal palaces (from the budget of the Department of Culture, Media and Sport) (text, page 235).

According to the Explanatory Notes accompanying it, the Sovereign Grant Act 2011 'develops a new streamlined system of support for Royal Household expenditure' for the monarch's official duties, and puts in place a new unified Sovereign Grant instead of the existing grants. The amount for the year 2012–2013 was set at £31 million (Sovereign Grant Act 2011, s 1(3)), with the amount in subsequent years to be determined by the royal trustees in accordance with a formula set out in the 2011 Act, s 6. The Sovereign Grant is paid from money provided by Parliament (s 1(6)).

There are now formal statutory obligations on the Royal Household to keep proper accounting records, which must be examined annually by the Comptroller and Auditor General, with a copy of the latter's report on the accounts (together with a statement of the accounts) to be submitted to Parliament by the Treasury (s 2). A Reserve Fund has been created, into which the Grant may be carried forward if unspent, and conversely from which any overspending can be drawn. The annual Grant is varied in accordance with a formula set out in s 6, and the formula itself can be varied by statutory instrument on a recommendation of the royal trustees (ss 7, 8).

Page 238
Personal prerogatives of the monarch

Dissolution of Parliament

As we have seen, the Conservative and Liberal Democrat parties negotiated an agreement for government and adopted a *Programme for Government* in the aftermath of the inconclusive general election in 2010. At the heart of that agreement was an unusual – if not unique – undertaking that the newly elected Parliament would serve a full term of five years. This would prevent either party from collapsing the Coalition at a time that seemed politically opportunistic, and would require both sides to enter into a constructive long-term relationship. This agreement led to the Fixed-term Parliaments Act 2011,[79] which declared not only that the date of the next general election is to be 7 May 2015 (s 1(2)), but also that all future general elections are to be held at fixed five-yearly intervals thereafter (s 1(3)).

This is an important provision that removes the right of the Prime Minister to choose the date of the general election:[80] that date has now been determined by the Coalition partners and is enshrined in law. However, it does not mean that there cannot be an early general election. In the first place, the Act provides that an election may be held following a House of Commons motion that there should be an early election if the motion is carried with the support of *two thirds of the number of seats* in the House (s 2(1),(2)). In the present House of Commons, the two parties to the Coalition have less than that number of seats, but if the Coalition were to break up, in circumstances where both Coalition parties wanted an early election, it seems unlikely in reality that Labour MPs would wish to oppose any such move.

In the second place, an early election can be held when a motion of no confidence is carried against the government in the Commons (passed by a *simple majority of those voting*), and this is not followed within 14 days by a motion of confidence in the government passed by a similar majority (s 2(3),(4)).[81] This period of 14 days would in theory enable a new government to be formed under a different leader if that government could then secure the support of a simple majority on the second vote. But again political reality makes this unlikely. So long as the Coalition agreement remains in place between the Conservatives and Liberal Democrats, a motion of no confidence could not be carried against the government. But if the Coalition breaks up, the likely result would be an early election.[82] If such an election is held, the new Parliament will last for a new five-year period before the next election is held (s 1(3)), not merely for the balance of the original five-year period.

---

[79] See M Ryan [2012] PL 213.
[80] On the power of the Prime Minister to advise the Queen on the date of the general election, see text, pages 240–242.
[81] As in 1979 when the Callaghan government resigned following a vote of no confidence.
[82] Subject to such possibilities as the Liberal Democrats agreeing to support a minority Conservative administration for a short period.

At first sight, the Fixed-term Parliaments Act 2011 may appear to be an import-ant constitutional innovation, in which a parliamentary decision requires a special majority to be effective. Although unprecedented, the possibility of something like this being done has been canvassed by constitutional scholars in the past.[83] However, the Fixed-term Parliaments Act 2011 can be repealed or amended in the same way as any other Act. As a result, the Act imposes a limit on the power of a Prime Minister only so long as future Prime Ministers are prepared to accept this limitation, provided of course they have a parliamentary majority to repeal the Act should they wish to do so. There is no suggestion of a special majority being required before the 2011 Act can be repealed or amended, though it is in any event unlikely that such a restriction could be legally effective.

In some political systems, there is an inflexible time-table of elections set by the constitution. But in the United Kingdom, the Fixed-term Parliaments Act 2011 appears to be nothing more than a legal device to cement the Coalition, in which the leader of the largest party in the Commons has effectively conceded the right to call a general election when it suits the interests of his party. As such, it is a major negotiating achievement of the Liberal Democrats and their leader Mr Clegg, who became Deputy Prime Minister in the Coalition. However, the 2011 Act is not binding on future Parliaments.[84] Although it might be difficult politically for a future government to bring forward a Bill to repeal the 2011 Act, it would always be possible to do so on the ground that the Act was addressed to a particular com-mitment in an agreement between two party leaders that was reached in private,[85] to overcome a unique political problem which each faced. More importantly, the 2011 Act does not stop the House of Commons elected in 2010 from removing the government if it were to lose the confidence of a majority of MPs.

Chapter 15

FOREIGN AFFAIRS AND THE COMMONWEALTH

Pages 316-320
Parliamentary approval to the ratification of treaties

Part 2 of the Constitutional Reform and Governance Act 2010, briefly mentioned in the text (at page 317, note 90), made an important reform in the process of

---

[83] See W I Jennings, *The Law and the Constitution* (5th ed, 1959), pp 145, 153, 161.

[84] By virtue of the doctrine of parliamentary sovereignty, it is elementary that no Parliament can bind its successors: see text, pages 60–63.

[85] The agreement in question being the Coalition agreement referred to above.

treaty-making that replaces the former practice followed under the so-called Ponsonby rule. The core of the new scheme for ensuring parliamentary approval to a treaty before it is ratified by the government is that a minister must lay the treaty in Parliament together with an explanation of the government's decision to ratify it; during the next 21 sitting days in Parliament, either House may resolve that the treaty be not ratified (2010 Act, s 20). When such a resolution is adopted by the House of Lords, the treaty may be ratified if the minister lays a further statement of why the treaty should nonetheless be ratified (s 20(8)).

In exceptional cases, a treaty may be ratified without it being laid in Parliament, but as soon as practicable a minister must lay the treaty before Parliament and explain why the normal process of prior laying had not been followed (s 22). Certain classes of treaty are not subject to this process, including EU treaties that by statute may be ratified only if first approved by Act of Parliament. For the purposes of the Act of 2010, the term 'treaty' means a written agreement (a) between states or between states and international organisations, that is (b) binding under international law; but it does not include regulations or rules made under the authority of a treaty (s 25).

This reform is to be welcomed in that it ensures that the two Houses know about treaties before they are ratified, even though this may come at a late stage in the process of treaty-making. The laying of a major treaty in Parliament should mean that the case for ratifying it will be examined by one or more committees at Westminster, but it is likely to be very rare for either House to resolve that a treaty may not be ratified. The scope of Part 2 of the 2010 Act is limited to dealing with parliamentary approval before ratification. The powers of the government to enter into and to ratify treaties are still derived from the royal prerogative.

Chapter 18

THE COURTS AND THE MACHINERY OF JUSTICE

Page 365
The judiciary and judicial appointments

The Crime and Courts Act 2013 makes many amendments to the Constitutional Reform Act 2005 that affect judicial appointments, particularly in relation to the question of diversity (text, page 368). The amendments are notable at least for their recognition of the existence of the problem, if not in the means taken to address it. In making judicial appointments on the grounds of merit, it is now provided that the relevant appointments commission (text, pages 365, 367) may make a choice between two candidates of equal merit 'for the purpose of increasing diversity' within the court to which the appointment is to be made. That is to say, where there are two equally meritorious candidates, one may be preferred on grounds of sex or race; but there is no obligation to use this power in any appointments recommended by the appointment commission in question. An important question arises about how this power will be used, and in particular whether it will be used consistently in all appointments. A new statutory duty requires both the Lord Chancellor and the Lord Chief Justice to 'take such steps' as they consider 'appropriate for the purpose of encouraging judicial diversity'.[86]

Contempt of Court and safeguards for the administration of justice

The Crime and Courts Act 2013 abolishes 'scandalising the judiciary' as a form of contempt of court under the common law of England and Wales. It had been generally thought that this form of contempt had fallen into disuse, but it reappeared when charges were brought in Belfast by the Attorney General of Northern Ireland against Peter Hain (former Secretary of State for Northern Ireland) about passages in his memoirs relating to the conduct by a High Court judge of a judicial review case in Northern Ireland. Mr Hain made it clear that he had no intention of undermining the administration of justice in Northern Ireland, saying that his words

> were never intended to, nor do I believe that they did, in any way undermine the administration of justice in Northern Ireland or the independence of the Northern Ireland judiciary, that very independence and integrity I worked so hard as secretary of state to achieve support for from all sections of the community, including those who had previously denied it.[87]

The charges were subsequently dropped, Mr Hain claiming a victory for free speech. Although 'astonishing', the charges were nevertheless a salutary warning, which led to calls that the 'ancient offence of scandalising a judge' should be 'confined permanently to history'.[88] In doing just that, however, the Crime and Courts Act 2013 applies only to England and Wales, and the abolition of scandalising the judiciary does not affect other aspects of the law of contempt, such as contempt in the face of the court that may involve the use of threatening words or scurrilous abuse (see text, page 376). It is also the case that defamatory statements about judges could lead to civil proceedings for libel brought by the judge in question.[89]

---

[86] Constitutional Reform Act 2005, s 137A, inserted by Crime and Courts Act 2013, Sch 13, Pt 2, para 11.
[87] *Guardian*, 17 May 2012.
[88] Ibid.
[89] K Dowell, 'Daily Telegraph Apologies to Sedley LJ Over Defamatory Allegations', *The Lawyer*, 9 March 2011.

Chapter 19

THE NATURE AND PROTECTION OF HUMAN RIGHTS

Page 397
The classical approach

At the time of the general election in 2010, there was some concern about the growing erosion of civil liberties and the need to roll back the power of the state.[90] These concerns were captured in the Coalition's *Programme for Government*, which included proposals to scrap the Labour government's ID card scheme and the National Identity register, and a commitment to regulate the use of CCTV and establish safeguards relating to the police DNA database. It was also proposed to 'restore' the right to non-violent protest, and to introduce safeguards against the misuse of anti-terrorism legislation, in a section of the *Programme for Government* reserved entirely for 'civil liberties'.[91] But while much of this was welcome, it should not be overlooked that several of the changes proposed were required as a result of· decisions of the European Court of Human Rights (for example on the DNA database, and the use of anti-terrorism legislation).[92] Many of the changes were introduced in the Protection of Freedoms Act 2012, considered more fully below.

Page 399
European Convention on Human Rights

Strong political opposition to the ECHR has led to calls for it to be renounced by the United Kingdom. But this seems unlikely to happen, if only because of its international repercussions, just as it is unlikely that the HRA will be repealed without being replaced by something substantially similar (see below). But human rights have been politicised not only in domestic law, with attempts also being made to take greater political control of the content of the Convention itself, and the manner of its operation and application. This is revealed most clearly by the political attacks on the Strasbourg Court in the British media and elsewhere, as well as by the political initiative in the form of the 'Brighton Declaration' designed to rein in the Court, an initiative taken at the time of the fortuitous British presidency of the Council of Europe in 2012.[93]

---

[90] For background to these measures, see K D Ewing, *Bonfire of the Liberties: New Labour, Human Rights and the Rule of Law* (2010).

[91] The Coalition, *Our Programme for Government*, above, p 11.

[92] *S and Marper v United Kingdom* [2008] ECHR 1581, (2009) 48 EHRR 50; *Gillan and Quinton v United Kingdom* [2009] ECHR 28, (2010) 50 EHRR 45.

[93] http://hub.coe.int/20120419-brighton-declaration. For discussion see, M Elliott [2012] PL 619.

One of the main thrusts of the 'Brighton Declaration', adopted at the 'High Level Conference on the Future of the European Court of Human Rights' in April 2012, is that member states and national courts should have primary responsibility for protecting Convention rights, subject to oversight from the Strasbourg Court. The objective is to be met in a number of ways, including revising the admissibility criteria,[94] and by amending the Convention to reinforce the Court's obligation to reinforce the principle of subsidiarity and the doctrine of the margin of appreciation in its jurisprudence, said to reflect the fact that 'the Convention system is subsidiary to the safeguarding of human rights at national level and that national authorities are in principle better placed than an international court to evaluate local needs and conditions'.[95]

From the point of view of constitutional principle, particularly noteworthy is the proposal for 'dialogue' between the Court and State Parties 'as a means of developing an enhanced understanding of their respective roles in carrying out their shared responsibility for applying the Convention'. This is to include 'dialogues' between the Court and:

(i)   The highest courts of the States Parties;
(ii) The Committee of Ministers, including on the principle of subsidiarity and on the clarity and consistency of the Court's case law; and
(iii) Government Agents and legal experts of the States Parties, particularly on procedural issues and through consultation on proposals to amend the Rules of Court.

It remains to be seen how this process evolves: will the dialogues be transparent? Will they take place in public? Will an account of the meetings be published? There may be a case for saying that if any dialogue is to take place between ministers and the Court, it should only be in the open forum of legal proceedings, not least because there would otherwise be a one-sided dialogue, with the Brighton Declaration making no provision for NGO's or victims' groups to be party to this proposed conversation on the construction of the treaty. It is in any event far from clear how far such an 'open dialogue' is consistent with the spirit of the Council of Europe's Recommendation on Judicial Independence of 2010,[96] an admirable

---

[94] Thus, 'an application should be regarded as manifestly ill-founded within the meaning of Article 35(3)(a), *inter alia*, to the extent that the Court considers that the application raises a complaint that has been duly considered by a domestic court applying the rights guaranteed by the Convention in light of well-established case law of the Court including on the margin of appreciation as appropriate, unless the Court finds that the application raises a serious question affecting the interpretation or application of the Convention'. The Court was also encouraged to have regard to the need to take a strict and consistent approach in declaring such applications inadmissible, clarifying its case law to this effect as necessary'.

[95] Some of these changes are captured by Protocol 15 to the ECHR adopted on 16 May 2013. For details see N. O'Meara, 'Reforming the European Court of Human Rights through Dialogue? Progress on Protocols 15 and 16 ECHR' UK Const L Blog (31 May 2013) (available at http://ukconstitutionallaw.org).

[96] Recommendation CM/Rec(2010)12 of the Committee of Ministers to Member States on Judges: Independence, Efficiency and Responsibilities: https://wcd.coe.int/ViewDoc.jsp?id=1707137.

document produced by the very governments who now appear to be unhappy with the Strasbourg Court.

While some of the concerns addressed by the Brighton Declaration are unexceptional, it is perhaps unsurprising that the manner by which others were addressed is said to have irritated the President of the Court, offended by politicians with a direct interest in the decisions of the Court telling the judges how to carry out their duties.[97] As already suggested, some of the proposals for treaty 'clarification' certainly reveal a poor understanding of the principle of judicial independence, and it is perhaps surprising that some of these proposals have not attracted more criticism. While the backlog in the Strasbourg Court provides a compelling case for radical procedural reform, there is also a compelling need to ensure that administrative expediency is not advanced at the cost of constitutional principle.

Page 407
The Human Rights Act 1998

Human rights are an area that has proved to be remarkably controversial in recent years, as well as being a subject about which the governing parties are split. Many on the Conservative side of the government appear hostile to both the ECHR and the Human Rights Act 1998; the Liberal Democrats generally support both. An attempt to reconcile these differences is to be found in the Coalition *Programme for Government*, in which the parties undertook to establish a commission to investigate the creation of a British Bill of Rights that 'incorporates and builds on all our obligations under the European Convention on Human Rights, ensures that these rights continue to be enshrined in British law, and protects and extends British liberties'.[98]

During the lifetime of the Coalition government, the differences between the two sides appear to have hardened, with some Conservatives speaking openly (if implausibly) about withdrawing from the Convention. Both the ECHR and the Human Rights Act are also the subject of extraordinary venom from vocal sections of the newspaper industry. Such rhetoric has been fuelled by decisions of the European Court of Human Rights with which both the government and the newspapers strongly disagree. Particularly significant have been the decisions discussed above that require a relaxation of the disenfranchisement of all prisoners[99] as well as the decision preventing the deportation of the radical preacher, Abu Qatada.[100]

Abu Qatada v *United Kingdom*[101] involved a terror suspect whom the United Kingdom government was prevented by the Court from deporting to Jordan. The

---

[97] J Rozenberg, 'Draft Brighton Declaration is a Breath of Fresh Air', *Guardian*, 19 April 2012.
[98] The Coalition, *Our Programme for Government*, above, p 11.
[99] See above, pages 14–15.
[100] *Othman v United Kingdom* [2012] ECHR 56, (2012) 55 EHRR 1; *Othman v Home Secretary* [2013] EWCA Civ 277.
[101] [2012] ECHR 56, (2012) 55 EHRR 1.

Court took the view that the deportation would contravene his Convention rights. Although he himself was unlikely to be tortured, there were concerns that he might be put on trial and that evidence obtained by torturing third parties would be used against him. The government's outrage at this decision appears to have been fuelled by the fact that the House of Lords had earlier rejected his claim that deportation in these circumstances would violate Convention rights.[102] It has thus been necessary for the Home Secretary to secure credible guarantees by means of a treaty with the Jordanian government that evidence obtained by torture would not be used in any trial of Abu Qatada.[103]

Even at the time it was established, it seemed unlikely that the Commission on a Bill of Rights would be able to resolve the sharp differences between the parties. Chaired by a retired senior civil servant and eventually composed exclusively of nine QCs, the Commission was unable to produce a unanimous report,[104] though it is true that seven of the nine were reported by one of their number to be 'in favour of a UK Bill of Rights written in language which reflects the distinctive history and heritage of the countries within the UK, and is different from the Human Rights Act'.[105] This appears to have alarmed the two prominent dissidents (at the time members of the Labour and Liberal Democratic parties respectively), who saw either a hidden agenda or unintended consequences, which would be a weakening of the impact of the ECHR in British law.

From the perspective of the government, however, this was probably not a failure. The existence of the Commission enabled a divisive issue to be addressed and managed if not resolved, and provided a blueprint for change that may be attractive to a Conservative government in the future, in order to deal with what would be a largely presentational replacement of the HRA with an alternative that would be substantially similar. The impact on domestic law of a replacement for the HRA would depend to a large extent on whether the United Kingdom remained a party to the ECHR, though even if the United Kingdom were to cease being a party to the Convention it by no means follows that ECtHR jurisprudence would cease to be influential in this country.[106]

Alongside the political debate on human rights, there is an on-going torrent of discussion in the courts and in legal literature about application of the Human Rights Act, the interpretation in United Kingdom courts of the Convention rights, and the relationship between those courts and the Strasbourg Court (see

---

[102] *RB (Algeria)* v *Home Secretary* [2009] UKHL 10, [2010] 2 AC 110.

[103] *BBC News*, 10 May 2013.

[104] The only non-QC member (apart from the Chair) was Dr Michael Pinto-Duschinsky. He resigned before the Commission reported: *The Guardian*, 11 March 2012. For the report, see Commission on a Bill of Rights, *A UK Bill of Rights? – The Choice Before Us* (2012).

[105] *BBC News*, 18 December 2012.

[106] For a good account of the complexity of some of the issues around the Commission's report and more generally, see H Fenwick, 'The Report of the Bill of Rights Commission: disappointing Conservative expectations or fulfilling them?', *UK Const L Blog* (21 March 2013) (available at http://ukconstitutionallaw.org).

text, pages 407–409). It is impossible here to summarise this rich abundance of materials, but one weighty contribution must be mentioned. Lord Irvine (who as Lord Chancellor was a principal architect of the Human Rights Act) has urged the Supreme Court to give s 2 of the Act its 'plain meaning' of requiring national courts to 'take into account' judgments of the Strasbourg Court, instead of holding that national courts are bound by judgments of that Court.[107] This argument that senior judges have been mistaken in their approach to the protection of human rights has not been found persuasive by other commentators.[108]

Chapter 20

CITIZENSHIP, IMMIGRATION AND EXTRADITION

Pages 429-430
Immigration Rules

Despite Lord Hoffmann's speech in *Odelola v Home Secretary* (text, page 429) examining the 'rather unusual' status of the Immigration Rules, disputes about the rules continue to arise. The disputes stem from disquiet about the substance of immigration policies, and the uneven practice of the Home Office in adopting new policies that affect the Immigration Rules themselves. In *Pankina v Home Secretary*,[109] the Home Office had issued 'policy guidance' that added an increased financial requirement to what the Immigration Rules said must be shown by students of UK universities who had come to study in the UK and wished to remain to do skilled work after graduating. The Court of Appeal held this requirement to be unlawful, since (as Sedley LJ said), the Immigration Rules 'have ceased to be policy and have acquired a status akin to law'. That additional requirement should have been laid before Parliament as an amendment to the Immigration Rules.

Not surprisingly, the implications of this decision were examined in a stream of other cases, culminating in two decisions by the Supreme Court. In *R (Munir) v Home Secretary*,[110] a Bangladeshi citizen and his wife and children were adversely affected by the withdrawal of a policy introduced in 1996 that enabled a family to remain in the UK where the children had had more than seven years' continuous residence. The policy and its withdrawal had never been included in Immigration

---

[107] Lord Irvine of Lairg [2012] PL 237.
[108] In particular by Sir Philip Sales [2012] 253. See also R Clayton [2012] PL 639.
[109] [2010] EWCA Civ 7191, [2011] QB 376.
[110] [2012] UKSC 32, [2012] 4 All ER 1025.

Rules. The Supreme Court rejected arguments for the Home Secretary that the power to make immigration rules was derived from the royal prerogative (see text, Chapter 12 D, E), but held that the policy in question did not have the nature of a rule and that neither the policy nor its withdrawal had to be included in the Immigration Rules. In R (Alvi) v Home Secretary,[111] the same court, grappling with the difficult borderline between what is and is not a rule that must be included in the Immigration Rules, held that 'the Immigration Rules should include all those provisions which set out criteria which are or may be determinative of an application for leave to enter or remain'.[112] Since some aspects of the 'points based system' for granting admission for certain occupations (text, page 430, note 118) were determinative of whether Alvi, an assistant physiotherapist, would be admitted, they should have been included in the Immigration Rules and not merely included in ancillary codes of practice.

Finally, the impact of the European Convention on Human Rights was felt in R (Quila) v Home Secretary:[113] an amendment to the Immigration Rules prevented married couples from living together in the UK where only one of the spouses was entitled to live in the UK, until both husband and wife were aged 21. The justification for the rule was said to be that it would have the effect of reducing the incidence of forced marriages, but the evidence of the likely effect was not convincing. The Supreme Court by 4-1 held that the age limit of 21 was a disproportionate interference with the rights of married couples under Article 8 ECHR (right to respect for private and family life).

On matters outside the Immigration Rules, difficulties arise over the status and application of Home Office policies. In R (Lumba) v Home Secretary),[114] several foreign national offenders who had been detained with a view to deportation after they had served their prison sentences challenged the unpublished policy of the Home Office, which applied a blanket presumption (contrary to the published policy) that such prisoners should be detained at the end of their prison sentences. The failure to publish the policy prevented the individuals from making meaningful representations against their detention. The Supreme Court held that the continued detention of the offenders was unlawful, but the nine judges were divided on the issue of whether damages should be paid for the unlawful detention, and (if payable) how they should be assessed. In a sequel to this case, the Supreme Court by 3-2 held in R (Kambadzi) v Home Secretary[115] that in exercising the statutory power to detain a foreign offender pending his deportation, the Home Secretary was under a public law duty to comply with the published policy contained in the Home Office's Operations Enforcement Manual. That policy required there to be regular reviews

---

[111] [2012] UKSC 33, [2012] 4 All ER 1041.
[112] Ibid, para [97].
[113] [2011] UKSC 45, [2012] 1 AC 621.
[114] [2011] UKSC 12, [2012] 1 AC 245 (the case was originally cited as *Abdi v Home Secretary*; see text, page 430, fn 119, and page 439, fn 201).
[115] [2011] UKSC 23, [2011] 4 All ER 975.

of K's continuing detention and these had not taken place. Lord Hope considered that 'a failure by the executive to adhere to its published policy without good reason can amount to an abuse of power which renders the detention itself unlawful'.[116] Lady Hale said: 'It is not statute, but the common law, indeed the rule of law itself, which imposes upon the Secretary of State the duty to comply with his own stated policy . . .'[117]

Pages 434-438
Refugees and asylum status

Many cases before the Supreme Court raise difficult issues in determining claims to asylum status. In *HJ (Iran) and HT (Cameroon)* v *Home Secretary*,[118] two gay men sought asylum on the basis that they had a well-founded fear of persecution if they had to return to their home countries, where they had been practising homosexuals. The Home Secretary accepted that homosexuals were a particular social group for the purposes of the Refugee Convention (text, p 435), but argued that they could reasonably be expected to tolerate the need to act discreetly in relation to sexual activity and thus avoid harm amounting to persecution. This 'reasonably tolerate' test, previously upheld by the Court of Appeal as being 'appropriate and workable', was rejected by the Supreme Court as being wrong in principle. It was one thing for a gay man to choose for social reasons to live discreetly (for instance, to avoid distress to his family), but if he had to live discreetly because of the fear of persecution from the state that would follow if he lived openly as gay, then he had a well-founded fear of persecution. In an eloquent judgment, the late Lord Rodger endorsed an Australian decision that rejected the 'reasonably tolerate' test: what the Convention protects is the right 'to live freely and openly as a gay man. This involves a wide spectrum of conduct, going well beyond conduct designed to attract sexual partners and maintain relationships with them. . . . [Gay] men are to be as free as their straight equivalents in the society concerned to live their lives in the way that is natural to them as gay men, without the fear of persecution'.[119]

A sequel to *HJ (Iran)* arose in the context of political freedom in *RT and KM (Zimbabwe)* v *Home Secretary*.[120] The evidence was that undisciplined militia supporting the regime in power in Zimbabwe were attacking persons returning from abroad, not only if they were known to be supporters of the opposition movement, but also if they did not demonstrate positive support for Zanu PF. The effect of these attacks was to cause someone who had never been politically involved to defend herself by giving lip-service to support for the Zanu PF regime. The Supreme Court held that the principle in *HJ (Iran)* 'applies to any person who has political

---

[116] Ibid, para [41].
[117] Ibid, para [73].
[118] [2010] UKSC 31, [2011] 1 AC 596.
[119] Ibid, para [78].
[120] [2012] UKSC 38, [2013] 1 AC 152.

beliefs and is obliged to conceal them' to avoid persecution, and also to a person 'who has no political beliefs and who . . . is forced to pretend that he does'. The human right to freedom of thought and expression extended to the freedom *not* to hold and *not* to have to express opinions, and (stressed Lord Dyson) was a key ingredient of human dignity. 'The idea "if you are not with us, you are against us" pervades the thinking of dictators.'[121]

Under the Refugee Convention, Article 1F (text, page 436), a person who faces a real risk of persecution if returned to their country is not protected if there are 'serious reasons for considering that . . . he has committed a crime against peace, a war crime, or a crime against humanity' as defined in international treaties. *R (JS, Sri Lanka) v Home Secretary*[122] concerned a Sri Lankan Tamil who had as a boy joined the Tamil Tigers and continued to be active in that body as an adult, taking part in military operations against the Sri Lankan army. In reviewing the international criminal case-law, the Supreme Court rejected the view that voluntary membership of an extremist group could in itself be presumed to amount to personal and knowing participation in crimes committed by the group. It was necessary to consider both the nature of the group's activities (did those activities constitute war crimes?) and the role that the individual played in the section of the group to which he belonged. In *Al-Sirri v Home Secretary*,[123] appeals by two asylum-seekers were against decisions based on Article 1F of the Refugee Convention, that there were serious reasons for considering that they had been 'guilty of acts contrary to the purposes and principles of the United Nations'. In interpreting the Refugee Convention, the Supreme Court took into account the Immigration, Asylum and Nationality Act 2006, s 54 and the EU Qualification Directive (text, page 437). It was held that Article 1F of the Refugee Convention should be 'interpreted restrictively and applied with caution', and that there should be a 'high threshold' in terms of the gravity of the acts in question. The requirement that there be serious reasons for considering a person to be guilty of such acts did not mean that that guilt must be proved beyond reasonable doubt; but it was unlikely that there would be sufficiently serious reasons for considering someone to be guilty unless the decision-maker could be satisfied on the balance of probabilities that he was.[124]

Pages 438-439
Deportation and removal from the United Kingdom

The courts deal with many situations in which a proposed deportation or removal that is otherwise lawful may breach the Convention rights of the individual or

---

[121] Ibid, para [44].

[122] [2010] UKSC 15, [2011] 1 AC 184.

[123] [2012] UKSC 54, [2013] 1 All ER 1267.

[124] See also *SK (Zimbabwe) v Home Secretary* [2012] EWCA Civ 807, [2012] 4 All ER 1205 (whether acts committed by Zanu PF youth militia in attacking white-owned farms were of a similar character to 'crimes against humanity').

their family members (text, page 439). In *ZH (Tanzania) v Home Secretary*,[125] a Tanzanian woman, whose claim for asylum had been refused, gave birth in the UK to children whose father was a British citizen and who therefore were also British citizens. If the mother were removed to Tanzania, the children were entitled to stay with their father or could accompany the mother, but on the evidence it was likely that they would have to go with her. The Supreme Court considered the weight that should be given to the best interests of the children (as required of the UK by the UN Convention on the Rights of the Child, 1989); the conclusion was that for the purposes of Article 8 ECHR (right to respect for private and family life) it would be disproportionate for the mother to be removed to Tanzania.

Pages 441-446
Extradition

It is evident from many cases that come to the courts that the procedure of the European Arrest Warrant (text, pages 443–444) presents some difficulties in practice for courts and prosecuting authorities in European countries. One notable decision of the Supreme Court arose from attempts by Julian Assange, an Australian citizen and the founder of Wikileaks, to avoid extradition to Sweden to be investigated on complaints against him by two women. As Sweden is a category 1 territory under the Extradition Act 2003, the extradition was sought by a European arrest warrant. In *Assange v Swedish Prosecution Authority*,[126] the Supreme Court by 5-2 held that the provision in the 2003 Act that the warrant must be issued by the competent 'judicial authority' of the state concerned could include in Sweden both a court and the public prosecutor. This broad meaning of 'judicial authority' was to be found in the EU Council's Framework Decision, to which Part 1 of the 2003 Act sought to give effect. The dissenting judges (Lady Hale and Lord Mance) emphasised that in UK law the term 'judicial authority' had a clear meaning that did not include a public prosecutor. They held that this narrower meaning should prevail, as the court was concerned with interpreting a UK Act of Parliament, in a matter that involved a serious interference with the right to liberty. Lord Mance supported this view with a close study of the debates on the Extradition Bill, made under the rule in *Pepper v Hart*.[127]

For both category 1 and category 2 countries, the Extradition Act requires the UK court to consider whether extradition of an individual would be compatible with his or her Convention rights (see text, page 443, note 229; and page 445, note 238).

---

[125] [2011] UKSC 4, [2011] 2 AC 66. For an assessment of proportionality on very different facts, see *UE (Nigeria) v Home Secretary* [2010] EWCA Civ 975, [2011] 2 All ER 352 (relevance of loss of some benefit to the community in Britain caused by an individual's removal).

[126] [2012] UKSC 22, [2012] 2 AC 471. The implications of this case were considered in *Ministry of Justice, Lithuania v Bucnys* [2012] EWHC 2771 (Admin), [2013] 1 All ER 1220.

[127] [1993] AC 593 (text, page 215).

In *Norris* v *United States Government (No 2)*,[128] a British businessman who faced serious charges of obstructing justice in the US argued that it would be disproportionate and a breach of his rights under Article 8 ECHR for him to be extradited; the nine-judge Supreme Court held that there was a public interest in the process of extradition such that it would only be the gravest effects of interference with family life that would be capable of rendering extradition to be disproportionate to the public interest.

In June 2011, the Joint Committee on Human Rights at Westminster criticised the UK's extradition policy for its failure adequately to protect human rights,[129] arguing that the threshold set by case-law such as *Norris* v *US Government (No 2)* was too high; the report also criticised the imbalance that existed under the UK's treaty with the USA (text, page 445). However, an independent review of the UK's extradition arrangements, chaired by Sir Scott Baker,[130] did not share these criticisms. Public concern over aspects of extradition reached a high level in the case of Gary McKinnon (text, page 445, note 238 and note 244), a young British man with Asperger's syndrome who had used his computer in London to gain access to US government computers. In October 2012, the Home Secretary decided that he should not be extradited to the USA. It was later stated that he would not be prosecuted in the UK for any offences, because of difficulties in securing evidence from the US.

Chapter 21

THE POLICE AND PERSONAL LIBERTY

Page 447
Organisation of the Police

Police and crime commissioners

A major development in relation to the police was the creation of directly elected police and crime commissioners (PCCs) by the Police Reform and Social Responsibility Act 2011. PCCs have a duty to 'secure the maintenance of the police force' for their area, and 'secure that the police force is efficient and effective' (Police Reform and Social Responsibility Act 2011, s 1(6)). He or she must hold the relevant chief constable to account, not only for the way in which the chief constable carries out his or her own functions, but also for the way in which those under the 'direction and control' of the chief constable carry out their functions (s 1(7)).

---

[128] [2010] UKSC 9, [2010] 2 AC 487.
[129] 'The Implications of the UK's Extradition Policy', HL Paper 156, HC 767 (2010–12).
[130] *Independent Review of the UK's Extradition Arrangements*, October 2011.

There is a PCC for each police area in England and Wales outside London, PCCs being directly elected to hold office for periods of up to four years. The first elections in 2012 were controversial, partly because the government refused to make available the means normally used at elections to enable candidates to communicate with electors by way of a free mail delivery.[131] The government's view was that this arrangement applies to parliamentary but not local elections, and that the PCC elections were of a local government rather than a parliamentary nature. Nevertheless, independent candidates in particular felt that they were at a disadvantage in what were large constituencies.

It is unlikely, however, that government parsimony in relation to electoral communications was the only reason for the very low turnout at the PCC elections, which at 15% across 41 police force areas is thought to be the lowest ever for any 'national' election in England and Wales.[132]

National Crime Agency

So far as national responsibility for policing is concerned, the Crime and Courts Act 2013 abolishes the Serious Organised Crime Agency (text, page 449) and creates a new National Crime Agency, with similar functions. Under the control of a Director General, the NCA has a number of functions, including what is referred to as a 'crime-reduction function', defined to mean the function of 'securing that efficient and effective activities to combat organised crime and serious crime are carried out', whether by the NCA itself or others (including other law enforcement agencies) (s 1). A second major function is a 'criminal intelligence function', defined to mean the function of 'gathering, storing, processing, analysing, and disseminating information' relevant to criminal activity of various kinds (s 1).[133]

The strategic priorities of the NCA are to be determined by the Home Secretary (s 3) in consultation with others,[134] including the Director General (who is appointed by the Home Secretary). The Director General in turn has wide powers to request – and ultimately to direct – chief constables in England and Wales to perform certain tasks set out in the request or direction. The Director General may only make requests (and not issue directions) to the newly created Police Service of Scotland, which is now the second largest police force in the United Kingdom with almost 25,000 police officers, staff and special constables.[135]

The provisions of the Crime and Courts Act 2013 apply to Scotland and Northern Ireland, as well as to England and Wales. However, an NCA officer may carry out certain activities in Scotland only with the agreement of the Lord Advocate.

---

[131] Representation of the People Act 1983, s 91.

[132] *BBC News*, 19 November 2012.

[133] These functions may be extended by order of the Home Secretary to include 'counter-terrorism' functions (s 2).

[134] They include so-called 'strategic partners', defined to include the Scottish Ministers, the Department of Justice in Northern Ireland, and representatives of local police forces (s 16).

[135] Police and Fire Reform (Scotland) Act 2012.

As stated in the text (page 452), the Serious Organised Crime and Police Act 2005 amended the law of arrest without a warrant. *Lord Hanningfield* v *Essex Chief Constable*[136] is a notable case in which the scope of these powers was tested. The applicant had recently been released from prison following a conviction relating to parliamentary expenses. Lord Hanningfield had been visited at home by five police officers at 6.45 am and arrested, following which his house was searched; he was then taken to a police station to be questioned about an offence relating to local government expenses when he had been leader of Essex County Council.[137]

The proper test to be applied in determining whether an arrest is necessary for the purposes of PACE 1984 s 24 is to be found in *Hayes* v *Chief Constable of Merseyside Police*,[138] where a 'two stage test' was proposed: (i) the constable actually believed that arrest was necessary, and for a reason prescribed by s 24(5); and (ii) objectively that belief was reasonable. In *Hanningfield*, Eady J held that 'the requirement of' necessity 'as laid down by Parliament has not, on any realistic interpretation of the word, been met'. The summary arrest was never going to have any impact on 'the prompt and effective investigation' of Lord Hanningfield's expenses, and there were 'no solid grounds to suppose that he would suddenly start to hide or destroy evidence, or that he would make inappropriate contacts'.

There was no justification 'for by-passing all the usual statutory safeguards involved in obtaining a warrant', with the result that Lord Hanningfield succeeded in his civil claim for damages for wrongful arrest. The wrongful nature of the arrest undermined both the legality of the search, as well as the legality of the detention at the police station. It is reported that Lord Hanningfield 'won' damages of £3,500.[139]

Page 459
Police powers of entry, search and seizure

Two decisions of the Administrative Court may have implications for police powers of search and seizure under PACE 1984, though the decisions in question did not directly concern the exercise of police powers under that Act. *Sher* v *Greater Manchester Chief Constable*[140] was concerned with the Terrorism Act 2000, Sch 8, which includes a power for magistrates to grant a search warrant. Although the granting of a search warrant is subject to judicial review on *Wednesbury* grounds,

---

[136] [2013] EWHC 243 (QB).
[137] The allegations were not pursued.
[138] [2011] EWCA Civ 911, [2012] 1 WLR 517.
[139] *BBC News*, 15 February 2013.
[140] [2010] EWHC 1859 (Admin), [2011] 2 All ER 364.

the application failed in circumstances that suggested that the court would give considerable leeway to the police. The warrant in that case was for one entry into the premises only, but the police entered the premises and remained there for several days. This was held not to be a breach of the warrant, the court taking the view that once on the premises the police may remain there until they have completed their task. It was also held that judicial review was not an appropriate remedy to challenge a wrongful arrest or unlawful detention by the police. This is because there are private law remedies for wrongful arrest and false imprisonment.

The other notable decision was R *(Dulai)* v *Chelmsford Magistrates Court*,[141] where a search warrant was issued to food inspectors under the Criminal Justice and Public Order Act 2001, s 50. The inspectors seized material on the premises but failed to comply with procedural obligations under the CJPOA 2001, s 52, which requires written notice to be given to the person from whom property has been seized. The Administrative Court reversed a decision of the Crown Court to quash the search warrant, on this occasion also applying *Wednesbury* to uphold the granting of the warrant. It was also held that the failure to comply with the procedural obligations in CJPOA 2001, s 52 did not invalidate the seizure. Rather, the failure on the part of the inspector to comply with these latter provisions was a matter to be taken into account by a court under PACE 1984, s 78 (text, page 470) in the event of any prosecution in which the contested material would be used as evidence.

Chapter 22

THE PROTECTION OF PRIVACY

Page 476

One of the more prevalent forms of surveillance in recent years has been the use of CCTV cameras and other devices used by public authorities to monitor people's behaviour. The use of such equipment may be governed by the Data Protection Act 1998, but it is not otherwise regulated by legislation devised for the purpose. A very small step in this direction is to be found in the Protection of Freedoms Act 2012, which requires the Home Secretary to prepare a Code of Practice ('the surveillance camera code') for the use of such equipment (s 29(1)), the code to be approved by Parliament (s 30). Specifically, the code should address the development or use of surveillance camera systems, as well as the use or processing of images or other information produced by such systems (s 29(2)). For these purposes, surveillance camera systems include both CCTV, and automatic number plate recognition systems (s 29(6)).

---

[141] [2012] EWHC 1055 (Admin), [2012] 3 All ER 764.

The code must address a number of matters prescribed by the PFA 2012. These include the circumstances in which it is appropriate to use surveillance camera systems, the types of systems or apparatus, the locations for systems or apparatus, access to, or disclosure of, information so obtained, and procedures for complaints or consultation (s 29(3)). The code will apply mainly to local authorities and the police ('relevant authorities'), which must have regard to the code when exercising any functions to which it relates (s 29). However, failure on the part of any person to act in accordance with any provision of the code 'does not of itself make that person liable to criminal or civil proceedings' (s 33(2)). The code is nevertheless admissible evidence in legal proceedings (s 33(3)), and a court or tribunal may take into account a failure by a relevant authority to have regard to the code in determining any question arising in the course of the proceedings (s 33(4)).

Provision is also made for the oversight of the new regime by the establishment of yet another Commissioner – the Surveillance Camera Commissioner. The latter will have responsibility to encourage compliance with the surveillance camera code, as well as to review its operation and provide advice about breaches and other matters (s 34). The Commissioner is to be appointed by the Home Secretary on terms determined by the Home Secretary (ibid), to whom he or she must report annually. These reports must be laid before Parliament and otherwise published by the Commissioner (s 35).

Page 477
Surveillance: acquiring information

Trespass

Concern about the large number of statutes conferring powers of entry on various public officials led to the introduction of remarkable provisions in the Protection of Freedoms Act 2012, in the Explanatory Notes to which it is claimed that there are over 1,300 pieces of primary or secondary legislation authorising state officials to enter private premises.

The 2012 Act confers new powers on the 'appropriate national authority', defined to mean a Minister of the Crown or the Welsh Ministers. Under these powers, the 'appropriate national authority' may by order 'repeal any power of entry or associated power which the appropriate national authority considers to be unnecessary or inappropriate' (s 39). It may also add safeguards of various kinds to existing powers (s 40) and, perhaps most remarkably, 'rewrite' such powers (s 41). A code of practice is to be issued to provide guidance relating to the power of entry (s 47).

Provision is also made in Sch 2 to repeal a number of existing powers of entry, though like most governments before it, the Coalition has found that it is expedient for it too to add to the existing powers of entry, notwithstanding the Protection of Freedoms Act 2012. Thus, the Scrap Metal Dealers Act 2013 provides that 'A constable or an officer of a local authority may enter and inspect a licensed site at any reasonable time on notice to the site manager' (s 16(1)). It also contains powers of entry without prior notice (s 16(2)), and additional powers of entry with a warrant (s 16(3)). Old habits die hard.

Surveillance and undercover operations

The Regulation of Investigatory Powers Act 2000 (RIPA) authorises the use of various surveillance practices by a wide range of public authorities (text, pages 480–481). The practices in question are referred to respectively as directed surveillance, intrusive surveillance and the conduct and use of covert human intelligence sources.[142] In the case of the first and third of these forms of surveillance, RIPA 2000 requires the need for authorisation before the power may be used, but also provides that the authorisation may be given by senior personnel within the agency conducting the surveillance.

In the case of local authorities (but not other agencies), amendments introduced by the Protection of Freedoms Act 2012 now require judicial approval before any such authorisation can take effect for either the first or third forms of surveillance (s 38, inserting a new s 32A in RIPA 2000).[143] In England and Wales, the approval is to be given by a justice of the peace, while in Scotland it is to be given by a sheriff and in Northern Ireland by a District Judge (Magistrates' Courts). It is provided that when an application is made for judicial approval of a surveillance authorisation, the applicant is not required to give notice of the application to any person to whom the authorisation relates, or to his or her legal representatives (RIPA 2000, s 32B(2)). To do so would defeat the purpose of the surveillance.

Page 492
Government databases

National Identity Register

The Identity Documents Act 2010 repealed the Identity Cards Act 2006. Identity cards already issued under the latter were cancelled by the former (s 2), which also requires the Home Secretary to ensure the destruction of all information held on the National Identity Register (s 3), for which there is now no legal authority. The 2010 Act re-enacted provisions of the Identity Cards Act 2006 relating to the possession of false identity documents. It also re-enacted measures imposing a duty on the part of specified persons to provide information to the Home Secretary, where this is required to verify information supplied by an applicant for a passport, or for the purposes of deciding whether a passport should be withdrawn from a passport-holder.

---

[142] On CHIS, see *Informer* v *Chief Constable* [2012] EWCA Civ 197, [2012] 3 All ER 601 (police owe duty of care to person engaged as an intelligence source to protect from harm; but no duty to protect from prosecution for offences committed).

[143] That is to say, directed surveillance or the conduct and use of covert human intelligence sources.

DNA Database

The Protection of Freedoms Act 2012 introduces important changes to the law relating to the retention of fingerprints and DNA profiles of people who have been arrested by the police but not charged, or who have been charged but acquitted. It was previously the case that, once taken, samples and profiles could be retained indefinitely, even in the case of those who were innocent. The Coalition *Programme for Government* included a commitment to 'adopt the protections of the Scottish model for the DNA database', a commitment to change the existing law being required as a result of the decision in *S and Marper* v *United Kingdom*,[144] where it was held that British practice at the time failed to meet the requirements of Article 8 of the ECHR, the Strasbourg Court rejecting the unanimous view of the House of Lords to the contrary.

Before the new law was introduced, however, steps were taken to test the implications of the *S and Marper* decision of the Strasbourg Court. In *R (GC)* v *Metropolitan Police Commissioner*,[145] one of the applicants was arrested but not charged with assault, and the other was charged but acquitted of rape. Both applicants had DNA samples taken under the authority of PACE, and both sought to have their records destroyed after the disposal of their cases. Although the Supreme Court declared the police procedures for the retention and use of DNA data to be unlawful, it nevertheless refused to order the destruction of the samples in view of the fact that Parliament was seised of the need to change the law, and that it would not be prudent to anticipate the forthcoming legislation by ordering the destruction of material the retention of which might be permissible in circumstances that would comply with Convention obligations.

Different categories of offence

The new law takes the form of a series of amendments to the Police and Criminal Evidence Act 1984 (see Chapter 21), for the purposes of which the legislation distinguishes between three different categories of offence, in what is a complex regulatory framework.

The first of the categories referred to in the PFA 2012 is that of **recordable offences**. This category is provided for in PACE, s 27, and refers to those offences that are recordable in national police records. This currently applies to (a) convictions for, and (b) cautions, reprimands and warnings given in respect of, any offence punishable with imprisonment and any offence specified in the schedule to the National Police Records (Recordable Offences) Regulations 2000 (as amended).[146]

The second category is that of **qualifying offences**, which is defined in PACE, s 65A, and applies to a list of scheduled offences, including murder, manslaughter, sexual offences, terrorist offences and many others.

---

[144] [2008] ECHR 1581, (2009) 48 EHRR 50.
[145] [2011] UKSC 21, [2011] 1 WLR 1230. See also *R (RMC)* v *Metropolitan Police Commissioner* [2012] EWHC 1681 (Admin) (retention of photographs).
[146] SI 2000 No 1139.

The third category is that of **excluded offences**, defined to mean a recordable offence which (i) is not a qualifying offence, (ii) is the only recordable offence of which the person has been convicted, and (iii) was committed when the person was aged under 18, and for which the latter was not given a custodial sentence of five years or more (broadly speaking, an offence committed by a minor who has not committed more than one offence).

The starting point of this new regime is the introduction of the new PACE, s 63D, which provides that fingerprints and DNA profiles (referred to hereafter as 'material') must be destroyed where they are unlawfully obtained or where they are obtained as a result of mistaken identity. In any other case, the material must be destroyed unless its retention is authorised by PACE, ss 63E to 63O, or some other unspecified legal power.

Grounds for retention

Investigation

The authorisations begin with cases **where the individual in question is under investigation by the police on suspicion of having committed an offence.** In these cases, the material 'may be retained until the conclusion of the investigation of the offence' or, where the investigation gives rise to proceedings against the person for the offence, until the conclusion of the proceedings (PACE, s 63E).

Arrested and/or charged but not convicted

Thereafter, it may be possible to retain the material of someone arrested or charged with a **qualifying offence**, even though the individual has not been convicted of the offence for which he or she has been arrested or charged (PACE, s 63F). Thus:

- in the case of someone with a previous conviction for a **recordable offence** (which was not an excluded offence), the material may be retained indefinitely (s 63F(2));
- in other cases, the material of a person who has been charged but not convicted of a **qualifying offence** may be retained for up to three years (PACE, s 63F);
- in the case of a person who has been arrested for a **qualifying offence** but not charged, material may be retained only with the consent of the Commissioner for the Retention and Use of Biometric Material.

This last power applies where the material was taken in the investigation of offences where the **victim** was under 18, a vulnerable adult, or closely associated with the suspect. An application may also be made to the Commissioner in relation to someone arrested for a **qualifying offence** where the retention of the material is 'necessary to assist in the prevention or detection of crime'. The individuals to whom the material relates must be given an opportunity to make representations to the Commissioner before any approval is given, unless his or her whereabouts are unknown (ss 63F, 63G).

In the case of those charged with but not convicted for, and those arrested but not charged in relation to, **qualifying offences**, the police may seek an extension of the three year period for another two years. The application must be made to a District Judge (Magistrates' Court), with a right of appeal by either party to the Crown Court against a refusal or granting of a renewal. Although it is not expressly provided that the hearing before the District Judge is *inter partes* (in contrast to the arrangements for an application to the Commissioner to retain the material in cases involving those arrested but not charged), the right of the individual must surely be implied (for example from the right to appeal), if not otherwise already provided for elsewhere.

In some cases, the material may be retained where it relates to an individual who has been arrested or charged but not convicted of a **recordable offence** (referred to in the side note as a 'minor offence'). In these cases, material taken or derived in relation to the investigation of the offence in question may be retained indefinitely if the individual arrested or charged (but not convicted) has a previous conviction for a **recordable offence** (which is not an excluded offence) (s 63H). This is in effect an authorisation based on an existing conviction, where the individual's material is not already retained.

Convicted

Otherwise, material taken or derived in the course of investigating a **recordable offence** may be retained indefinitely in the case of someone convicted of the offence in question (s 63I). In the latter case, there is an exception for persons under the age of 18, provided the offence is not a **qualifying offence** and the convicted person has not previously been convicted of another **recordable offence** (s 63K).[147]

Other matters

The foregoing thus provides a regime for the indefinite retention of the DNA profiles of anyone convicted of a recordable offence, as well as in some cases of those who have been arrested for or charged with a qualifying or recordable offence, even though the individual in question has not been charged and even though the individual has been charged and found not guilty. For these purposes, a conviction is widely defined to include a caution in respect of an offence which the person admitted having committed, a warning or reprimand to a young person issued under the Crime and Disorder Act 1998, s 65 for the offence in question, a finding of not guilty by reason of insanity, and the finding that a person has been found to have committed an offence while under a recognised legal disability (s 65B).

Further provision is made for cases where the individual has received a penalty notice (s 63L), where the retention of the material is deemed necessary for reasons of national security (s 63M), and where the information was given voluntarily

---

[147] Where this proviso applies, the material may be retained indefinitely in the case of those given a custodial sentence of five years or more; in other cases, the material may be retained for the length of the custodial sentence plus five years, or for five years in the event of a non-custodial sentence.

(s 63N), or retained with consent (s 63O). National security allows material to be retained for renewable periods of two years following a determination by the chief officer of police. The exercise of this power must take place only in accordance with guidelines issued by the Home Secretary, in preparing which the minister must consult with both the Commissioner for the Retention and Use of Biometric Material and the Lord Advocate,[148] the former being a newly created office with general powers of oversight.

Apart from thus determining from whom samples may be taken and profiles retained (on the National DNA Database),[149] the Act determines the purposes for which the data may be used. These are: (a) in the interests of national security, (b) for the purposes of a terrorist investigation, (c) for purposes related to the prevention or detection of crime, the investigation of an offence or the conduct of a prosecution, or (d) for purposes related to the identification of a deceased person or of the person to whom the material relates (s 63T). Questions also arise about the content of the existing National DNA Database at the time the Protection of Freedom Act 2012 comes into force, with s 25 providing that the Home Secretary must provide for the destruction or retention of material obtained before the commencement day.

However, it seems that not **all** existing material needs to be destroyed, and it may be assumed from s 25 that material relating to those who have been convicted will not be destroyed. The Act expressly permits the retention of existing material in the case of people who have been arrested or charged but not convicted of a qualifying offence. Material must be destroyed if taken or derived three years or more before the commencement day. However, where the material was taken or derived less than three years before the commencement day, it may be retained for up to three years from the date when it was taken or derived. In the case of non-qualifying offences, material taken or derived before the commencement date must be destroyed (if it relates to someone arrested or charged but not convicted).

Chapter 23

FREEDOM OF EXPRESSION

Page 518
Defamation

The Defamation Act 2013 makes important changes to the law of defamation, so far as it affects freedom of expression. Perhaps most importantly, by virtue of s 1, a statement is now not defamatory unless its publication has 'caused or is likely

---

[148] Protection of Freedoms Act 2012, s 22.
[149] Ibid, s 23.

to cause serious harm to the reputation of the claimant' (s 1(1)).[150] Even more important for those engaged in campaigns against large companies in particular, it is provided that 'harm to the reputation of a body that trades for profit is not "serious harm" unless it has caused or is likely to cause the body serious financial loss' (s 1(2)).

Apart from tightening up on the nature of the harm that must be established, the 2013 Act also amends the law relating to defences. Section 2 abolishes the common law defence of justification (text, page 519) and replaces it with a new truth-based defence, which applies where the 'imputation conveyed by the statement complained of is substantially true' (s 2(1)). Where a statement is capable of two or more distinct imputations, the defence applies if one is substantially true and any other is not, provided that the latter does not cause any substantial harm. In addition to abolishing the defence of justification, the 2013 Act also abolishes the common law defence of fair comment, replacing it with a new defence of honest opinion (s 3(1)),[151] which applies where three conditions are met: the statement complained of was a statement of opinion (s 3(2)); the statement complained of indicated the basis of the opinion (s 3(3)); and the opinion is one that could have been held by an honest person on the basis of any fact existing at the time of the publication, or anything asserted as a fact in a privileged statement (s 3(4)).

Section 4 abolishes the so called *Reynolds* defence, which was established in a decision bearing the same name (text, pages 521–522) and further refined in *Flood* v *Times Newspapers Ltd.*[152] There is a new statutory defence in its place, designed ostensibly to codify the common law rules in force at the time of enactment. The new defence may be engaged where a contested statement (a) was, or formed part of, a statement on a matter of public interest, which (b) the defendant reasonably believed it was in the public interest to publish.[153] The scope of the statutory defence is said to reflect the common law defence it replaced, and to embrace both an objective (part (a)) and a subjective (part (b)) element. In determining 'whether it was reasonable for the defendant to believe that publishing the statement complained of was in the public interest' (part (b)), the court is required to 'make such allowance for editorial judgment as it considers appropriate' (s 4(4)). It is also provided 'for the avoidance of doubt' that the new defence under s 4 may be relied upon 'irrespective of whether the statement complained of is a statement of fact or a statement of opinion' (s 4(5)).

---

[150] A statement for these purposes is defined to mean 'words, pictures, visual images, gestures or any other method of signifying meaning'.

[151] See *Joseph* v *Spiller* [2010] UKSC 53, [2011] 1 AC 852, where it was thought that the common law defence of fair comment should be renamed honest comment. For the position in Scotland, see *Massie* v *McCaig*, 2013 CSIH 13 (allegedly defamatory remarks about the purpose of a political donation).

[152] [2012] UKSC 11, [2012] 2 AC 273.

[153] There is no definition of public interest for these purposes, though the Explanatory Notes accompanying the Act make clear that 'the current case law would constitute a helpful (albeit not binding) guide to interpreting how the new statutory defence should be applied. It is expected the courts would take the existing case law into consideration where appropriate' (para 35).

Additional measures provide a defence for internet operators, who may escape liability if they can show that they did not post the offending statement, though the defence may be defeated if the operator fails to remove the offending statement (s 5). There is also protection for work published in peer-reviewed scientific or academic journals (s 6), which is now privileged in the absence of malice. Amendments are made to the Defamation Act 1996, s 14 in relation to the law of privilege, to extend the existing protection of absolute privilege for the fair and accurate reporting of legal proceedings; and to extend the existing protection of qualified privilege on a number of grounds, including the 'fair and accurate report of proceedings at a press conference held anywhere in the world for the discussion of a matter of public interest'.

While the foregoing provisions address concerns about the substance of the law, other measures in the Defamation Act 2013 address procedural points, designed in part to respond to concerns about 'libel tourism', whereby someone with a remote connection with the United Kingdom sues for defamation in the English courts when only a few copies of an allegedly defamatory article have been published in this country. Steps to tighten up on this are in the 2013 Act, s 9. In these cases, a defamation action may not be brought unless 'the court is satisfied that, of all the places in which the statement complained of has been published, England and Wales is clearly the most appropriate place in which to bring an action in respect of the statement' (s 9(2)). As explained in the Explanatory Memorandum accompanying the Act, 'where a statement has been published in this jurisdiction and also abroad the court will be required to consider the overall global picture to consider where it would be most appropriate for a claim to be heard'.[154]

Three other procedural changes are also significant. The first is the abolition of jury trial in defamation cases (s 11), an issue that has been a major concern for publishers over many years. The second is the power of the court to require a summary of its judgment in a defamation case to be published by the defendant. Where the parties are unable to agree the content of the summary, the dispute may be resolved by the court (s 12(3)), which may give directions about 'the time, manner, form or place of publication' if necessary (s 12(4)).[155] The third procedural change

---

[154] The Explanatory Notes give by way of example a statement 'published 100,000 times in Australia and only 5,000 times in England', which would be 'a good basis on which to conclude that the most appropriate jurisdiction in which to bring an action in respect of the statement was Australia rather than England'. However, a number of factors would have to be taken into account in addition to the number of times a statement was published in different jurisdictions, 'including, for example, the amount of damage to the claimant's reputation in this jurisdiction compared to elsewhere, the extent to which the publication was targeted at a readership in this jurisdiction compared to elsewhere, and whether there is reason to think that the claimant would not receive a fair hearing elsewhere'.

[155] Section 12 complements and extends generally the provisions of the Defamation Act 1996, s 8, which gives the court in some circumstance the power to deal with defamation cases by way of summary judgment. In these cases the court could order the defendant to publish a suitable correction and apology (s 9(1)(b)). If the parties are unable to agree the content of any such correction or apology, 'the court may direct the defendant to publish or cause to be published a summary of the court's judgment agreed by the parties or settled by the court in accordance with rules of court' (s 9(2)). Where the parties are unable to agree on the time, manner, form or place of publication of the correction and apology, 'the court may direct the defendant to take such reasonable and practicable steps as the court considers appropriate' (ibid).

is to be found in s 13, which applies where a court gives judgment for the claimant, in circumstances where the defendant may not be in a position to require the offending material to be withdrawn from circulation (as where it is on an internet site, or is being distributed by others). In such cases, the court may order the removal of a defamatory statement from a website; it may also order a person other than the author, editor or publisher of the statement to stop distributing, selling or exhibiting material containing the statement (s 13(1)).

Chapter 24

FREEDOM OF ASSOCIATION AND ASSEMBLY

Page 529
The right of public meeting

The Police Reform and Social Responsibility Act 2011, s 141 repealed the provisions of the Serious Organised Crime and Police Act 2005 relating to demonstrations in the vicinity of Parliament (text, page 529). They have been replaced by new controls on activities in Parliament Square Garden and the adjoining pavements (Police Reform and Social Responsibility Act 2011, ss 142–149). With the activities of recent anti-war protestors clearly in mind, the new legislation is designed to stop the unauthorised use of loudspeakers and loudhailers, and the use of tents and sleeping equipment in the controlled area. Police officers have wide powers to give directions to individuals to cease a prohibited activity, failure to comply with which is an offence (s 143).[156] It is permissible to use these powers against someone who had previously been authorised to do that which now constitutes a controlled activity.[157]

Page 538
Public order offences

By virtue of the Crime and Courts Act 2013, s 57, it is no longer an offence under the Public Order Act 1986, s 5 to use 'insulting' words or behaviour, or to distribute or display writing, signs, or other visible representations on the ground only that they are 'insulting'. Section 5 applies where the words or behaviour on the one hand, or the writing, signs, or other visible representations on the other, are used within the hearing of any person likely to be caused harassment, alarm or distress. There is thus no need for there to have been any intention to cause harassment,

---

[156] On the scope of the powers, see ss 144, 145.
[157] R *(Gallastegui)* v *Westminster City Council* [2012] EWHC 1123 (Admin), [2012] 3 All ER 401.

alarm or distress; nor is it necessary that anyone has suffered harassment, alarm or distress, though it is a defence for the accused to show that he or she 'had no reason to believe that there was any person within hearing or sight who was likely to be caused harassment, alarm or distress' (s 5(3)(a)).

This small change to the 1986 Act was initiated in the House of Lords. It was initially resisted by the government, which thought the offence of using insulting words or behaviour was useful to deal with people who desecrated poppies on Remembrance Day or swore at police officers, and it was also used against Christian fundamentalists who railed against homosexuality. This power to prosecute for insulting behaviour alone was thought by some to be an unjustifiable restraint on free speech, though it was defended by the police as being a valuable tool to help them keep the peace and maintain public order, and others saw it as a way of protecting minorities. Despite this amendment to the 1986 Act, it is to be emphasised that the use of insulting words or behaviour and the delivery of insults by means of writing, signs or other visible representations continues to be unlawful where it falls within the 1986 Act, sections 4 and 4A (on which see the text, pages 540–541).

Page 545
Preventive powers of the police

The controversial police practice of containment of demonstrators was considered by the European Court of Human Rights in *Austin* v *United Kingdom*,[158] following the decision of the House of Lords in *Austin* v *Metropolitan Police Commissioner*.[159] The main question for the Court was whether the detention of the complainants amounted to a deprivation of liberty under Article 5 ECHR, in which case it might have been difficult for the government to claim that the restriction was justified by reference to Article 5(1)((a)–(f), which does not appear to make provision for preventive powers of the police of this kind. By a majority, however, the Court sidestepped the problem by saying that the detention was a restriction on freedom of movement rather than a deprivation of liberty.

It is true that the majority accepted that 'the coercive nature of the containment within the cordon; its duration; and its effect on the applicants, in terms of physical discomfort and inability to leave Oxford Circus, point towards a deprivation of liberty' (para 64). But the Court also accepted that it must take into account 'the context in which the measure was imposed', noting that 'the measure was imposed to isolate and contain a large crowd, in volatile and dangerous conditions', and that 'the police decided to make use of a measure of containment to control the crowd, rather than having resort to more robust methods, which might have given rise to a greater risk of injury to people within the crowd' (para 66). The decision that there was no deprivation of liberty was 'based on the specific and exceptional facts' of the case (para 68).

---

[158] [2012] ECHR 459, (2012) 55 EHRR 14.
[159] [2009] UKHL 5, [2009] AC 564.

The complainants did not argue that there had been a breach of their rights under Articles 10 and 11 ECHR, but the majority nevertheless reiterated that 'measures of crowd control should not be used by the national authorities directly or indirectly to stifle or discourage protest, given the fundamental importance of freedom of expression and assembly in all democratic societies' (para 68).

Chapter 26

EMERGENCY POWERS AND PREVENTION OF TERRORISM

As discussed in Chapter 26 of the text, several provisions of the Terrorism Act 2000 were very controversial. These included the power to detain terrorist suspects for up to 28 days before charge (text, page 594), the power of the police to invoke and exercise stop and search powers where 'expedient for the prevention of acts of terrorism' (text, page 595), and the power of the Home Secretary to restrain individuals by means of control orders to protect the public from the risk of terrorism (text, pages 598–599). So far as the first of these matters is concerned, the Protection of Freedoms Act 2012 introduced simple amendments to the Terrorism Act 2000 reducing the length of pre-charge detention to a maximum of 14 days (s 57) (though there are also provisions to enable the 28 day period to be reinstated in urgent circumstances when Parliament is dissolved, there presumably being no need for such powers when Parliament is in session).[160] The response to the other two matters is slightly more complicated.

Page 593
Terrorist investigations and counter-terrorist powers

So far as the powers of the police to stop and search are concerned, the Protection of Freedoms Act 2012, s 59 repealed the controversial Terrorism Act 2000, ss 44–47. This followed the decision of the Strasbourg Court in *Gillan and Quinton* v *United Kingdom*[161] that the provisions in question violated the ECHR, Article 8(1) and could not be justified under Article 8(2) (text, page 595). But although repealed, the offending provisions of the 2000 Act were replaced by a new Terrorism Act 2000, s 47A, with more tightly drawn powers that the government presumably believes will now be consistent with its Convention obligations.

---

[160] Protection of Freedoms Act 2012, inserting a new Terrorism Act 2000, Sch 8, Part 4. A number of safeguards have been introduced to contain the exercise of this power should it ever be reinstated.
[161] [2009] ECHR 28, (2010) 50 EHRR 45.

The replacement power provides that stop and search may be invoked by the authorisation of a senior police officer who (a) 'reasonably suspects that an act of terrorism will take place', and (b) 'reasonably considers' that the authorisation is 'necessary to prevent such an act'. There are tighter geographical and temporal factors now to be considered in making an authorisation, in the sense that the area covered must be no greater than necessary to prevent the suspected act of terrorism, while the duration of the authorisation must be no longer than necessary (s 47A(1)). Once made, the authorisation empowers a constable in uniform to stop a vehicle in the specified place and to search the vehicle, its driver and passengers, and anything else in the vehicle (s 47A(2)).

Moreover, an authorisation enables a constable in uniform to stop and search a pedestrian, and to search anything the pedestrian may be carrying (s 47A(3)). In both cases, the replacement power retains an equivalent to the original legislation restricting the power of stop and search to 'be exercised only for the purpose of searching for articles of a kind which could be used in connection with terrorism' (s 47A(4)). Crucially, however, 'the power conferred by such an authorisation may be exercised whether or not the constable reasonably suspects that there is such evidence' (s 47A(5)). It is thus the case that the 2012 amendments retain the power of random stop and search, which was perhaps the greatest departure in the Terrorism Act 2000, s 45 from what was referred to by Lord Brown in *R (Gillan)* v *Metropolitan Police Commissioner* as 'our traditional understanding of the limits of police power'.[162]

Further provisions relating to the power of stop and search are to be found in the Terrorism Act 2000, Sch 6B, also introduced by the 2012 Act (s 61(2), Sch 5). This deals with the way in which the power is exercised (no removal of any clothing in public except for headgear, footwear, an outer coat, a jacket or gloves); and the obligation to provide a written statement relating to the exercise of the power (to be provided only on request within 12 months of the incident). An authorisation is now valid for only 14 days, unlike the previous provisions by which the authorisation was valid for up to 28 days. Like the provisions it replaces, however, the new law provides for renewal of an authorisation, provided that the tighter grounds for invoking the power have been met. Consistently with the requirements of the replaced provisions, an authorisation by a senior police officer is valid for only 48 hours unless confirmed (with or without modifications) by the Home Secretary.

Page 596
Detention without trial, control orders and secret justice

Control orders were introduced by the Prevention of Terrorism Act 2005, and were the subject of important decisions of the House of Lords and the Supreme Court. Most recently in *Home Secretary* v *AP*,[163] the person subject to a control order with a 16-hour detention requirement was subsequently required to live some 150 miles away from his family to avoid contact with 'radical elements'. The Supreme Court

---

[162] [2006] UKHL 12, [2006] 2 AC 307.
[163] See text, pp 599–600. See also [2011] 1 AC 1.

53

upheld a Divisional Court decision to quash this requirement, holding that restrictions on private life can be taken into account in determining that in exceptional cases the circumstances give rise to a violation of Article 5 of the ECHR. The Supreme Court also suggested that the higher courts should respect the expertise of the Administrative Court in this field.

Although the 2005 Act has been repealed, the Terrorism Prevention and Investigation Measures Act 2011 reintroduced provisions similar to control orders, though not quite as restrictive. Under the replacement provisions, the Secretary of State may issue a notice of temporary protection and investigation measures (a 'TPIM notice'), provided conditions A to E in s 3 are met. These are respectively that:

(Condition A) the Secretary of State reasonably believes that the individual is, or has been, involved in terrorism-related activity (the 'relevant activity').

(Condition B) some or all of the relevant activity is new terrorism-related activity.

(Condition C) the Secretary of State reasonably considers that it is necessary, for purposes connected with protecting members of the public from a risk of terrorism, for TPIMs to be imposed on the individual.

(Condition D) the Secretary of State reasonably considers that it is necessary, for purposes connected with preventing or restricting the individual's involvement in terrorism-related activity, for the specified TPIM to be imposed on the individual.

(Condition E) a court gives the Secretary of State permission to impose a TPIM notice, unless he or she reasonably considers that on grounds of urgency TPIMs should be imposed without such permission.

TPIM notices may be imposed for a period of up to a year, though they may be renewed by the Home Secretary (on one occasion only), provided that conditions A, C and D above are met.

The normal procedure for the imposition of a TPIM is for an application to be made by the Home Secretary to the High Court, which must consider whether any decisions of the minister relating to the application are 'obviously flawed',[164] and whether to grant permission for the measures to be imposed on the individual. It is provided that the court may consider the application in the absence of the individual; without the individual having been notified of the application; and without the individual having been given an opportunity of making any representations to the court (s 6(4)). The Act then provides that in determining an application for a TPIM, 'the court must apply the principles applicable on an application for judicial review' (s 6(6)), having just enacted that the proceedings can be conducted in breach of one of these principles, namely the requirement of procedural propriety. An application may be granted only if the court concludes that the Home Secretary's decisions in relation to Conditions A, B and C are not 'obviously flawed'. However, a finding that a decision in relation to Condition D is obviously flawed does not mean that the application cannot be granted, the court being empowered to give directions to the Home Secretary about the measures to be imposed on the individual (s 6(10)).

---

[164] Specifically, the decisions relating to Conditions A, B, C and D.

Although a TPIM notice may thus be issued in the absence of the respondent, provision is made for the review of such notices by a court in his or her prescence; this is to occur 'as soon as reasonably practicable' (s 8). The purpose is to review the decisions of the Home Secretary that 'the relevant conditions were met and continue to be met' (s 9(1)). In performing this role, the court must again comply with the principles of judicial review (s 9(2)), and in doing so may quash the TPIM notice; may quash measures specified in the TPIM notice; and may give directions to the Home Secretary in relation to revocation of the TPIM notice, or the variation of measures specified therein (s 9(5)). Otherwise, the court must decide that the notice is to continue in force (s 9(6)). These powers may be exercised only after the Home Secretary has consulted the police about the possibility of criminal charges being brought against a person in respect of whom TPIM measures are contemplated (s 10). Where a TPIM notice is issued, the police should be informed by the Home Secretary, and steps should be taken by the police to 'secure that the investigation of the individual's conduct, with a view to a prosecution of the individual for an offence relating to terrorism, is kept under review throughout the period the TPIM notice is in force' (s 10(5)(a)).

Although the 2011 Act includes ostensibly more robust safeguards for the individual than the control order regime it replaced, no one should be under any illusion about the substance of the powers conferred on the minister. The 12 categories of restraint provided for in the Act relate to what are referred to as overnight residence measures, travel measures, exclusion measures, movement directions measures, financial services measures, property measures, electronic communication device measures, association measures, work or study measures, reporting measures, photography measures, and monitoring measures. These are largely self-explanatory, though a fair amount of detail relating to the scope of each is provided for in the Act. It would not be appropriate necessarily to apply all of these measures to everyone who is the subject of a TPIM notice: to do so would be a violation of Condition D and would invite more carefully targeted measures being imposed by the High Court (though of course it is always open to a minister to test the court by taking measures greater than might be required by the circumstances). But they are nonetheless formidable powers.

Chapter 28

DELEGATED LEGISLATION

Pages 626-627
Authority to modify an Act of Parliament

Despite constitutional criticism, the Coalition government follows its predecessors in expecting Parliament to confer power on ministers to modify Acts of Parliament.

The Public Bodies Act 2011, giving effect to a Cabinet Office review of public bodies in 2010, is a controversial example of this practice.[165] It conferred power on ministers to abolish bodies specified in Sch 1 to the Act and to transfer their powers to 'eligible persons' such as UK Ministers, Scottish and Welsh Ministers and 'any other person exercising public functions' (s 1). Schedule 1 to the Act included bodies such as the Administrative Justice and Tribunals Council, the Commission for Rural Communities, the Inland Waterways Advisory Council, the Library Advisory Council for England, and the National Consumer Council. The Act conferred power to merge bodies listed in Sch 2 (including the Competition Commission and the Office of Fair Trading) and to change the constitutions of other public bodies. The Act includes several restrictions on use of the powers: s 7 seeks to protect functions such as judicial and enforcements powers that must be exercised independently of ministers, s 10 requires prior consultation, and s 11 enables use of the Act to be subject to an enhanced affirmative procedure that can be triggered by either House, similar to that in the Legislative and Regulatory Reform Act 2006 (text, pages 626–627, 630). While such powers may be effective in pruning public bodies that have become 'dead wood' since they were created, the Act was in 2013 used to abolish the Administrative Justice and Tribunals Council when the overwhelming evidence was that it was still needed (see comment on Chapter 29, Administrative Justice, below).

Pages 634-636
Judicial review of delegated legislation

In *Ahmed v HM Treasury*,[166] the Supreme Court held ultra vires clauses in Orders in Council made under the United Nations Act 1946 that sought to implement resolutions of the UN Security Council requiring states to freeze the assets of persons who *commit or attempt to commit* terrorist acts. One reason why the orders were ultra vires was that they went wider than the Security Council resolutions by being stated to apply where there were '*reasonable grounds for suspecting*' that someone was or might be a terrorist; also, the effect of one order was to deprive an individual of the chance to seek judicial review of his or her listing as a terrorist. In *R v Forsyth*,[167] concerning another Order in Council made under the 1946 Act, it was claimed that the order was invalid because it had been made ten years after the Security Council had asked governments to prevent funds being made available to Iraq. The Supreme Court held that, while urgent measures would often be required

---

[165] For criticism of the original Bill, see 6th report, Select Committee on the Constitution (HL Paper 51 2010–12). See also 50th report, Merits of Statutory Instruments Committee (HL, Paper 250, 2010–12). And Cabinet Office, *Using the Public Bodies Act 2011*, March 2012.

[166] [2010] UKSC 2, [2010] 2 AC 534 (cited as *HM Treasury v Mohammed Jabar Ahmed* at text, page 635, fn 94). See also, the same parties, *(No 2)* [2010] UKSC 5, [2010] 4 All ER 829 where the court refused by 6-1 to suspend the immediate effect of the first decision.

[167] [2011] UKSC 9, [2011] 2 AC 69.

by the Security Council, the lapse of time did not prevent the government from implementing this Security Council resolution.

An Iranian bank suspected of being involved in financing Iran's nuclear programme challenged a Treasury Order made under the Counter-Terrorism Act 2008 that effectively excluded the bank from the UK financial market.[168] It was held that, although a different order could have been made that would have had less effect on the bank, the order served a legitimate aim that affected the national interests of the UK, and the Treasury was entitled to exercise a wide margin of appreciation. In a case arising from a Security Council Resolution concerning the supply of military equipment to Iraq, an Order in Council was held not to be effective, since an essential definition of the banned equipment could not be found in other delegated legislation; criticising government departments for not keeping proper records of their legislation, the Court of Appeal refused to supply its own definition to fill the gap in the prosecution's case.[169]

A regulation made by the Lord Chancellor introducing a new scheme of costs for criminal legal aid was held to be unlawful, since the relevant Act required the amount payable to be what the court considered 'reasonably sufficient' to compensate lawyers for expenses properly incurred, and it was not a legitimate goal for the minister to try to bring down market rates by regulations that did not comply with the statute.[170] The Lord Chancellor was also held to have had an improper purpose when he wished to amend the Legal Services Commission Funding Code to restrict applications for judicial review against the Ministry of Defence: Laws LJ said, 'For the state to inhibit litigation by the denial of legal aid because the court's judgment might be unwelcome or apparently damaging would constitute an attempt to influence the incidence of judicial decisions in the interests of government. It would therefore be frankly inimical to the rule of law'.[171]

Pages 636-638
Administrative rule-making

This complex phenomenon of modern government provided the backcloth for the decisions concerning Immigration Rules and immigration policies that have already been discussed (see commentary on Chapter 20, above). As those cases indicate, a public authority that has adopted and published a certain policy comes under a duty in law to apply the policy. This position was exemplified in R (Davies) v Revenue and Customs Commissioners,[172] where the Revenue had published a booklet that offered general guidance on the meaning of 'residence' and 'ordinary

---

[168] Bank Mellat v HM Treasury [2011] EWCA Civ 1, [2012] QB 101.

[169] R v v D [2011] EWCA Crim 2082, [2012] 1 All ER 1108.

[170] R (Law Society of England and Wales) v Lord Chancellor [2010] EWHC 1406 (Admin), [2011] 1 All ER 32.

[171] R (Evans) v Lord Chancellor [2011] EWHC 1146 (Admin), [2011] 3 All ER 594, para [25].

[172] [2011] UKSC 47, [2012] 1 All ER 1048.

residence', dealing with basic issues of tax law that determine whether individuals are subject to being taxed in the UK. The taxpayers claimed that a revised version of the booklet gave a more benevolent interpretation than previously of the relevant rules, but that the new interpretation was not being applied in practice. The Revenue accepted that *if* the booklet had given such an assurance, the taxpayers must succeed, on the basis of their legitimate expectation that the Revenue would give effect to that assurance (see text, pages 697–703). However, the Revenue argued that the booklet could not be properly read as having the meaning favoured by the taxpayers. The Supreme Court criticised the drafting of the booklet in some respects, but by 4-1 upheld the Revenue's interpretation of the booklet, if read as a whole by someone described as an 'ordinarily sophisticated taxpayer'.

Since a public authority must give effect to policies that it has adopted, questions may arise as to whether a particular policy has been adopted. *R (K)* v *Birmingham Council*[173] concerned the difficult situation that arises when a person seeking asylum claims to be under 18 (on which basis he would come under the care of the local social services authority) but the local authority believes him to be over 18 and thus subject to immigration control as an adult, administered by the Home Office. In 2005, a protocol had been agreed between the Immigration Directorate of the Home Office and the Association of Directors of Social Services that provided a procedure to be followed when an applicant's age was in dispute. The Court of Appeal held, on the evidence, that the Birmingham council had not adopted the protocol as its policy and had not sought to follow it. It was thus not at fault for failing to comply with the protocol.

Chapter 29

ADMINISTRATIVE JUSTICE

Pages 640-647
Tribunals

The radical reorganisation of the system of tribunals that was authorised by the Tribunals, Courts and Enforcement Act 2007 (text, pages 644–646) is now firmly established. The new structure of tribunals was brought even closer to that of the civil and criminal courts, with the creation in 2011 of Her Majesty's Courts and Tribunals Service (HMCTS), an executive agency within the Ministry of Justice. It is unfortunate that the government saw the reformed tribunal structure as providing an opportunity for abolition of the Administrative Justice and Tribunals Council, (text, pages 646–647) which had under the Act of 2007 replaced the Council on

---

[173] [2012] EWCA Civ 1432, [2013] 1 All ER 945.

Tribunals, created in 1958. In the opinion of the government, '[the] independence of the tribunal system administered by HMCTS ensures that tribunal members and the administrative support systems are sufficiently removed from decision makers to diminish the need for a standing body to oversee tribunals'.[174] This view was not shared by those who saw the Council as committed to ensuring the independence of tribunals and also maintaining the quality of administrative justice in general. The abolition of the Council, along with its Scottish and Welsh committees, was to be achieved by means of subordinate legislation, subject to parliamentary procedure, under the Public Bodies Act 2011 (see comment on Chapter 28 above).[175]

Under the Tribunals, Courts and Enforcement Act 2007 which created the First-tier Tribunal and the Upper Tribunal (text, page 645), appeals may be brought from the First-tier Tribunal to the Upper Tribunal on a point of law, but only if leave is given by either Tribunal. From the Upper Tribunal, an appeal may with permission be brought on a point of law to the Court of Appeal in England and Wales (and in Scotland to the Court of Session). In two Supreme Court cases heard together in 2011, *R (Cart)* v *Upper Tribunal* and *Eba* v *Advocate General for Scotland*,[176] the question arose whether, if leave to appeal is refused by both First-tier and Upper Tribunals, that refusal is subject to judicial review. The Divisional Court in *Cart* had rejected the argument that, because the 2007 Act described the tribunal as a 'superior court of record', the Upper Tribunal's decisions were not subject to judicial review. The Court of Appeal held further that the Upper Tribunal did not have the status of the High Court, even though High Court judges might sit in the Tribunal. The Supreme Court in *Cart* held that (a) the Upper Tribunal's decisions were subject to judicial review, but (b) in light of the tribunal structure under the 2007 Act, it was reasonable to restrict judicial review by applying criteria that in civil procedure now apply to limit the making of a 'second-tier appeal' to the Court of Appeal, and also to appeals from the Upper Tribunal to the Court of Appeal. These criteria are (a) that the appeal raises an *important point of principle or practice* or (b) that there is *some other compelling reason* for the appeal to be heard.[177] In reaching this decision, the Supreme Court emphasised both the importance of entrusting the courts with authority to uphold the law, and the need for courts to remember that even in the administration of justice, resources are limited. In *Eba* v *Advocate General for Scotland*,[178] a similar conclusion was reached for Scotland (text, pages 724–726); and the Supreme Court ruled that, contrary to what was held in *Watt* v *Lord Advocate*,[179] (text, page 724) the Scottish

---

[174] 32nd report of Secondary Legislation Scrutiny Committee (2012–13, HL Paper 146).

[175] See the Public Bodies (Abolition of the Administrative Justice and Tribunals Council) Order 2013. The draft Order was strongly criticised at Westminster (see eg 21st report of Public Administration Select Committee (HC 1621, 2010–12) and 8th report of Justice Select Committee (HC 965, 2010–12)) but the government did not withdraw it.

[176] Respectively [2011] UKSC 28, [2012] 1 AC 663; and [2011] UKSC 29, 2011 SLT 768.

[177] Access to Justice Act 1999, s 55(1); Tribunals, Courts and Enforcement Act 2007, s 13(6).

[178] [2011] UKSC 29 2011 SLT 768.

[179] 1979 SC 120.

courts may correct an error of law made by a statutory tribunal even if the error might be said to be 'within jurisdiction'. Lord Hope observed that, while the position of tribunals in Scotland has not been identical with their position in English law, the 2007 Act did apply to Scotland and there were common factors (such as the need to respect the expertise of specialist tribunals) that indicated that Scots law and English law should now be aligned.

The broad area of administrative justice continues to feel the impact of Article 6(1) ECHR, which guarantees the right to a fair and public hearing by an independent and impartial tribunal in the determination of civil rights and obligations and of criminal charges. As stated in the text (page 647), the First-tier and Upper Tribunals can be expected to comply fully with Article 6(1) and for this reason disputes are unlikely to arise as to whether these tribunals are determining civil rights and obligations within the meaning of Article 6(1). But questions about such compliance can arise when there is a decision-making procedure outside the main structure of tribunals: it may then be necessary for the court to decide (taking account of the complex Strasbourg case-law on Article 6(1)), (a) whether the procedure involves a determination of 'civil rights and obligations' and, if so, (b) whether Article 6(1) has been observed.

In *Ali* v *Birmingham Council*,[180] under housing legislation a council ceased to be under a duty to find housing for a homeless person when she had refused an offer of suitable accommodation that had been made to her. If she contested the decision that she had refused such an offer, she could ask the council to review that decision, but otherwise had only an appeal on law to the county court. The Supreme Court held that the decision that she had refused a suitable offer of housing did not engage Article 6(1), since that decision involved a series of evaluative judgments on a matter that was outside the category of 'civil rights'. In *R (G)* v *Governors of X School*,[181] the issue was whether, at a disciplinary hearing by school governors of a charge that a teaching assistant had an inappropriate relationship with a 15-year-old boy, the assistant was entitled to be represented by a solicitor. A dismissal for this reason would be reported to the Secretary of State and would lead to a procedure before an independent agency with power to ban the assistant from working with children. It was argued for G that the governors' decision on the facts would have such a strong influence on the assessment of facts during the agency's procedure that he had a right under Article 6(1) to be legally represented before the governors. The Supreme Court by 4-1 rejected this argument, holding that the agency must make its own decision on facts that were disputed. In *Mattu* v *University Hospitals of Coventry*,[182] the Court of Appeal held that disciplinary proceedings conducted by an NHS trust into the performance of a consultant's contract would not bar him from being employed elsewhere as a consultant and did not involve the determination of his 'civil rights'.

---

[180] [2010] UKSC 8, [2010] 2 AC 39.

[181] [2011] UKSC 30, [2012] 1 AC 167.

[182] [2012] EWCA Civ 641, [2012] 4 All ER 359. See also *R (King)* v *Justice Secretary* [2012] EWCA Civ 376, [2012] 4 All ER 44 (prison governor's decision to confine prisoner to cell for breach of prison discipline held by 2-1 not to involve determination of prisoner's 'civil rights').

The account of the Ombudsman in the text refers more than once to the outstanding work as Parliamentary and NHS Ombudsman of Ms Ann Abraham (and see text, page 659, note 121). In October 2011, she delivered the annual Tom Sargent lecture for JUSTICE, entitled 'The Ombudsman and Administrative Justice' and available on the Ombudsman's website, which summarised her views on the constitutional role of the Ombudsman and emphasised the need for some reforms. In January 2012, she was succeeded as Ombudsman by Dame Julie Mellor.[183]

The need for greater integration in the system of public sector ombudsmen was identified by a Cabinet Office review in 2000 (text, page 668), but this led only to limited changes. The Law Commission returned to this matter in 2008 (text, page 746) in the consultation paper, *Administrative Redress: Public Bodies and the Citizen*, dealing with ombudsmen in the broad context of remedies against public authorities. In 2010, the Law Commission accepted that its attempts to reform the judicial remedies available in administrative law would not succeed, and restricted its final report on administrative justice to reforms in the system of public sector ombudsmen.[184] The Commission's recommendations included provisions for facilitating access to ombudsmen (by enabling complaints to be made other than in writing, and by repealing the 'MP filter' for complaints to the Parliamentary Ombudsman), for widening the discretion of ombudsmen to deal with complaints which might also give rise to a remedy in the courts, and empowering the Administrative Court to issue a stay on judicial review proceedings to enable the appropriate ombudsman, if he or she chose, to investigate the complaint. Other changes proposed were to enable an ombudsman to refer a question of law to the Administrative Court and to publish more information about his or her investigations and findings, but without identifying individuals concerned except with their consent.

Chapter 30

JUDICIAL REVIEW OF ADMINISTRATIVE ACTION I

Pages 671-673
The ultra vires rule (excess of powers)

Some new illustrations of the ultra vires rule come from local government, which was formerly subject to much stricter rules than are considered desirable today. In

---

[183] For her first annual report to Parliament, see HC 251 (2012–2013).
[184] *Administrative Redress: Public Bodies and the Citizen* (2010, Law Com 322), HC 1136 (2010–12).

one well publicised case, R *(National Secular Society)* v *Bideford Town Council*[185], it was held that the council had no power under s 111, Local Government Act 1972 to hold Christian prayers as part of a formal council meeting: the holding of prayers could not be regarded as conducive to or incidental to the transaction of council business, since councillors were entitled to choose not to attend this part of the meeting. One effect of the Localism Act 2011 is to make it less likely that such illustrations will arise in future. By s 1(1) of the Act, 'A local authority has power to do anything that individuals generally may do' and, by s 1(2), 'this applies to things that an individual may do even though they are in nature, extent or otherwise (a) unlike anything the authority may do apart from subsection (1), or (b) unlike anything that other public bodies may do'. However, later provisions in the Act concern the 'boundaries of the general power'. In particular, the general power does not release the authority from statutory restrictions that already apply to the authority; but by s 5, the Secretary of State has power to make delegated legislation removing such restrictions, subject to observing a parliamentary procedure similar to that under the Legislative and Regulatory Reform Act 2006 (text, page 626). Other limitations on the new general power of local authorities apply to the manner in which they may do things for commercial purposes (2011 Act, s 4). The new power does not permit councils to act in breach of rights under the ECHR or to adopt discriminatory measures that are in breach of equality legislation.

Pages 674-676
Irrelevant considerations and improper purposes

Two examples have already been given of measures adopted by the Lord Chancellor which were held to be unlawful because they had been in part motivated by an irrelevant consideration and an improper purpose.[186] In R *(FDA)* v *Work and Pensions Secretary*[187] the Secretary of State decided by an order made under the Pensions (Increase) Act 1971 to change the basis for calculating the annual up-rating in public sector pensions from the Retail Price Index, which had previously been used, to the Consumer Price Index. The CPI was likely to produce a lower average price increase than the RPI, and thus a lower annual increase in pensions. Public sector trade unions challenged the change on several grounds, claiming that the Secretary of State had taken into account irrelevant considerations, namely his concern about the economy and the impact of the change on the national exchequer. It was held that, although the Secretary of State must ensure that his decision on up-rating conformed to what he was required to do by the Act of 1971, he could make a rational choice in selecting the appropriate index; since the decision involved was

---

[185] [2012] EWHC 175 (Admin), [2012] 2 All ER 1175.
[186] See comments on Chapter 28 above, concerning R *(Law Society of England and Wales)* v *Lord Chancellor* and R *(Evans)* v *Lord Chancellor*.
[187] [2011] EWCA Civ 332, [2012] 3 All ER 301.

macro-economic in character, Lord Neuberger MR said that it would be unrealistic to require the Secretary of State 'to ignore the wider economic realities' [para 61].

Pages 683-684
The concept of jurisdiction

In R v *Home Secretary, ex parte Khawaja*,[188] the House of Lords upheld the principle that, where the exercise of executive power depends on 'the precedent establishment of an objective fact', a court must if necessary decide for itself whether that requirement has been satisfied. In R *(A)* v *Croydon Council*,[189] this principle was invoked before the Supreme Court, to govern the situation in which a young asylum-seeker claimed to be under the age of 18, but the social services authority decided after assessing the individual that he was over 18. It was held that in the case of such disputes the court must itself decide the issue of age, and it was not sufficient for the court to find that there were reasonable grounds for the decision. Referring to the Children Act 1989, Lady Hale said that the word 'child' was defined 'in wholly objective terms (however hard it may be to decide upon the facts of the particular case)'. 'This is an Act for and about children. If ever there were a jurisdictional fact, it might be thought, this is it.'[190] Lord Hope said: 'The scheme of the 1989 Act shows that it was not Parliament's intention to leave this matter to the judgment of the local authority'.[191]

Pages 688-690
The rule against bias

In *Porter* v *Magill*[192] (text, page 688) Lord Hope held that a judge should be disqualified from acting when 'the fair-minded and informed observer, having considered the facts, would conclude that there was a real possibility that the tribunal was biased'. This formulation continues to be the governing principle that applies to cases of alleged bias in a judicial context, and significant instances of its application have arisen in relation to the role of the judge and of a juror in criminal trials.[193]

---

[188] [1984] AC 74.
[189] [2009] UKSC 8, [2010] 1 All ER 469.
[190] Ibid, para [32].
[191] Ibid, para [53]. And see R *(K)* v *Birmingham Council*, cited above in comment on Chapter 28 (administrative rule-making).
[192] [2001] UKHL 67, [2002] 2 AC 357.
[193] See in particular R v S [2009] EWCA Crim 2377, [2010] 1 All ER 1084 (judge disqualified by possibility of apparent bias from proceeding to conduct the trial without a jury when under the Criminal Justice Act 2003 the jury was discharged on grounds of jury tampering, and the judge had previously conducted nine trials involving the same defendant) and A G of Cayman Islands v *Tibbetts* [2010] UKPC 8, [2010] 3 All ER 95 (appeal on ground that verdict of jury should be set aside when one juror had previous friendship with a prosecution witness: held that the 'fair-minded and informed observer' should consider the nature of that friendship and also whether the jury's acceptance of the prosecution evidence might have been affected by that friendship).

Two cases of alleged bias in the conduct of disciplinary proceedings had contrasting outcomes. In *Virdi* v *Law Society*,[194] proceedings for professional misconduct were brought against a solicitor: the tribunal appointed under the Solicitors Act 1974 found the charges proved and barred him from practice for three years. The solicitor appealed, claiming that it had been unlawful and unfair for the clerk of the tribunal to accompany the tribunal when it retired to deliberate on its decision, and for the clerk to take part in recording the decision of the tribunal. The Court of Appeal held that the hypothetical informed observer was not restricted to publicly available information, and could be assumed to be fully informed of the facts and of any explanation given by the tribunal. On the evidence the tribunal had acted properly. And the fact that the clerk was an employee of the Law Society was not significant, since she worked solely for the tribunal, and the Society's judicial functions had been delegated to the tribunal, which was 'not in any relevant sense an agent of the Law Society'.[195] By contrast, in *R (Kaur)* v *Institute of Legal Executives Appeal Tribunal*,[196] a student member of the Institute of Legal Executives (ILEX) had been found guilty on charges of 'conduct unbefitting to ILEX or likely to bring ILEX into disrepute' for allegedly cheating in an ILEX examination. Her appeal to the ILEX Appeal Tribunal was rejected. One member of the appeal tribunal was the vice-president of ILEX. The Court of Appeal held that the vice-president had an interest in ILEX's policy of disciplinary regulation and was disqualified by her leading role in ILEX from sitting on the tribunal. Rix LJ said that the case demonstrated 'the importance of proper separation of the disciplinary panels from those concerned with the overall governance of the organisation'.[197]

Pages 686-687
Statutory requirements

The principle laid down in *R* v *Soneji*[198] (text, page 687) that applies when a court must decide the effects of non-compliance with a statutory procedure was followed in *R (Herron)* v *Parking Adjudicator*.[199] In a challenge to the imposition of parking charges in the city of Sunderland, it was claimed that various irregularities in the display of signs designating the streets subject to parking restrictions meant that no parking infringements had occurred. The Court of Appeal held that the test for invalidity was whether there had been substantial compliance with the relevant statutory requirements; the evidence was that drivers were adequately informed of the parking restrictions, and accordingly there was no good reason for holding the parking scheme to be invalid.

---

[194] [2010] EWCA Civ 100, [2010] 3 All ER 653.
[195] Ibid, para [47].
[196] [2011] EWCA Civ 1168, [2012] 1 All ER 1435.
[197] Ibid, para [52].
[198] [2005] UKHL 49, [2006] 1 AC 340.
[199] [2011] EWCA Civ 905, [2012] 1 All ER 709.

Chapter 31

JUDICIAL REVIEW OF ADMINISTRATIVE ACTION II

Pages 721-722
Statutory exclusion of judicial control

In *A v B (Investigatory Powers Tribunal)*,[200] A, a former member of the Security Service, wished to publish a book about his work in the service and had to seek consent from the Service to do so. Permission to publish parts of the manuscript was refused and A sought judicial review of that refusal, relying on his rights under Article 10 ECHR. The Supreme Court held that, under the Regulation of Investigatory Powers Act 2000, it was only the Investigatory Powers Tribunal (text, page 558) that had jurisdiction to deal with A's case. The 2000 Act said expressly that the Investigatory Powers Tribunal was 'the only appropriate tribunal' for the purposes of proceedings against the Security Service that relied on the Human Rights Act. The effect of the relevant legislation was to bring A's claim within the principle applied in *Barraclough v Brown*[201], and (distinguishing *Anisminic Ltd v Foreign Compensation Commission*[202]) it was not open to the court to interpret the legislation so as to maintain the possibility of judicial review. Lord Brown said: 'Parliament has not ousted judicial scrutiny of the acts of the intelligence services; it has simply allocated them to the Investigatory Powers Tribunal.'[203]

Pages 726-729
Habeas corpus

One consequence at a global level of the fears for national security arising from the 9/11 attacks on the USA in 2001 is the practice of 'rendition' (text, page 446), sometimes called 'extraordinary rendition', by which persons suspected of links with terrorism are transferred between states and may be held for years without trial. The ancient process of habeas corpus has been invoked both in the USA[204] and in the United Kingdom in attempts to subject rendition to the rule of law. In *Rahmatullah v Foreign Secretary*,[205] Rahmatullah, a citizen of Pakistan, had in February 2004 been detained by British forces serving in Iraq. He was handed over

---

[200] [2009] UKSC 9, [2010] 2 AC 1.
[201] [1897] AC 615 (statute creating a duty and providing a means of enforcing it). And text, page 709.
[202] [1969] 2 AC 147: text, page 721.
[203] [2009] UKSC 9, para [23].
[204] See *Boumediene v Bush* 553 US 723 (2008).
[205] [2012] UKSC 48, [2013] 1 All ER 574.

to American forces and taken to the Bagram airbase in Afghanistan, where he was detained. In 2010, a US review board determined that he was not 'an enduring security threat' and that he should be released to Pakistan. But by October 2012, he was still detained. On Rahmatullah's behalf, habeas corpus was sought in the English courts against the British Foreign and Defence Secretaries; it was argued that his detention was unlawful and that the Secretaries had retained a sufficient degree of control over him to secure his release. This degree of control arose from a Memorandum of Understanding between the US, UK and Australian governments in 2003 which stated that transfer of prisoners of war and civilian detainees between the three states must comply with the relevant Geneva Conventions; it provided that someone (such as Rahmatullah), detained by UK forces, 'will be returned' by the US to the UK 'without delay upon request' by the UK.

The seven judges in the Supreme Court held unanimously that there was prima facie evidence that Rahmatullah was illegally detained and that, even though the Secretaries of State did not have physical control of him, there were grounds on which they could claim to assert control, such that there was a reasonable prospect that they could produce him to the court. These grounds arose from the Memorandum of Understanding in 2003 and the UK's obligations under the Geneva Conventions. For the court to order the Secretaries of State to make a return to the writ of habeas corpus did not involve the court in intruding upon issues of foreign policy and diplomacy. However, it was also held (by 5 judges to 2) that a sufficient return to the writ had already been made by the Secretaries of State, as they had made clear the US view that R's continued detention was lawful and that if he were to be released, he would be released to Pakistan. Lady Hale and Lord Carnwath dissented: in their view, 'the strength of habeas corpus is its simplicity'; 'detention once established is presumed to be illegal until the contrary is shown by the detainer or the person allegedly in control'. If R had not been handed over to the US forces, he would have been released long ago. 'Where liberty is at stake, it is not the court's job to speculate as to the political sensitivities which may be in play.'[206] In this minority view, the Secretaries of State should be ordered to request the US authorities to transfer Rahmatullah back to UK custody, in conformity with the Memorandum of Understanding of 2003.

The outcome was that the UK courts provided no tangible support for someone detained without trial for over 8 years, most of that time outside the UK's jurisdiction. A key question not addressed in the judgments is how the Memorandum of Understanding could create rights and obligations in the absence of an Act of Parliament to give it the force of law. But the judges must have had in mind the Geneva Conventions Act 1957, s 1, which makes a grave breach of the relevant Conventions a criminal offence.[207]

---

[206] Ibid, paras [121], [129].
[207] Ibid, para [6].

Chapter 32

LIABILITY OF PUBLIC AUTHORITIES AND THE CROWN

Pages 734, 752
Tort liability of the Crown towards the armed forces

As stated on page 734 (and see page 338), the Crown Proceedings (Armed Forces) Act 1987 suspended operation of s 10 of the Crown Proceedings Act 1947, which restricted the Crown's liability for death or personal injury caused to members of the armed forces by other members. The 1987 Act authorises s 10 of the 1947 Act to be brought back into effect in certain circumstances, but this has not been done as regards operations in Iraq and Afghanistan.[208] In *R (Smith) v Defence Secretary*,[209] a member of the Territorial Army serving in Iraq died of hyperthermia, after reporting sick because of the heat. At an inquest held in the United Kingdom, there were procedural defects. Smith's family sought a fresh inquest, relying on the guarantee for the right to life given by Article 2 ECHR, which requires a state to hold a full inquiry in certain instances of death. The issue before the Supreme Court was whether for purposes of the ECHR, Smith was within the 'jurisdiction' of the United Kingdom. The court held, by 6-3, that a soldier of a European state serving abroad was not within the jurisdiction of his or her state for the purposes of Article 1 ECHR, despite the soldier's undoubted status in national law.

The decision of the majority is a very difficult one. As Lord Phillips recognised in the leading judgment, 'Under domestic law and in accordance with public international law, members of the armed forces remain under the legislative, judicial and executive authority of the United Kingdom, whether serving within or outside the United Kingdom.'[210] But in his view the issue was what the parties to the ECHR intended when they agreed to Article 1 ECHR. In dissenting judgments, Lords Mance and Kerr asked rhetorically whether, if British soldiers serving in Iraq 'were not within the jurisdiction of the United Kingdom, in whose jurisdiction were they?'[211] It must be emphasised that the decision did not concern the tort liability of the Ministry of Defence, although reference is made to the Crown Proceedings Act.[212] But the remarkable effect of the majority decision was that, while an Iraqi

---

[208] As to which, see *Mulcahy v Ministry of Defence* [1996] QB 732, discussed at text, page 339.
[209] [2010] UKSC 29, [2011] 1 AC 1.
[210] Ibid, para. [53].
[211] Ibid, para. [318] (Lord Kerr) and [191] (Lord Mance).
[212] Ibid, para. [189] (Lord Mance) and [240] (Lord Collins). In *Smith v Ministry of Defence* [2012] EWCA Civ 1365, [2013] 1 All ER 778, on actions under the Crown Proceedings Act 1947 arising from the death or injury of British soldiers in Iraq, the Court of Appeal struck out claims based on the ECHR, but allowed claims of negligence to proceed. On appeal, the Supreme Court applied the Strasbourg Court's approach in *Al Skeini v UK* (2011) 53 EHRR 589, and held that British soldiers in Iraq were within UK Jurisdiction for Convention purposes: [2013] UKSC 41.

citizen who was detained by British soldiers in Iraq and brutally assaulted by them was for ECHR purposes within the jurisdiction of the United Kingdom,[213] soldiers who have been maltreated by other soldiers while in Iraq have no human rights claim against the government, even if they can sue the MoD in tort.

Pages 735-736
Statutory authority as a defence

In *Barr* v *Biffa Waste Services*,[214] the Court of Appeal held that claimants who lived near a landfill site, where a statutory permit for tipping 'pre-treated waste' had been issued by the Environment Agency, were entitled to sue the operators in nuisance when the process at the site created seriously unpleasant smells that interfered with the claimants' comfortable enjoyment of their land. The court applied established principles of the law of nuisance, and rejected the argument that use of the landfill site was reasonable and that the operators could be liable only if they were shown to be negligent in conduct of the site.

Pages 736-738
Statutory duties

Two decisions of the Court of Appeal provide further instances of the need for a court to decide whether a statutory duty is enforceable by an action for damages (text, page 737). In *Poulton's Trustee in Bankruptcy* v *Ministry of Justice*,[215] in breach of the Bankruptcy Rules county court officials failed to notify the Chief Land Registrar of a bankruptcy petition issued in the court; the result was that the petition was not included in the register of pending actions, and the bankrupt person was able to sell land and deprive her creditors of the proceeds. It was held that the Bankruptcy Rules did not disclose an intention that failure to perform the rules should result in a private claim for damages. In *Ali* v *Bradford Council*,[216] a pedestrian who slipped on a public footpath that she claimed was obstructed by mud, vegetation and rubbish, sued the highway authority for personal injuries resulting from a breach of its duty under the Highways Act 1980, s 130, to prevent, as far as possible, the obstruction of highways. It was held that s 130 was concerned with enabling the general public to have right of access to public highways and did not give rise to a duty to prevent and remove obstructions to the highway.

---

[213] *R (Al-Skeini)* v *Secretary of State for Defence* [2007] UKHL 26, [2008] 1 AC 153 (text, pages 340–341). In *Al Skeini* v *UK* (2011) 53 EHRR 589, the Strasbourg Court held that all the Iraqi claimants were in the Jurisdiction of the UK (Art 1, ECHR).
[214] [2012] EWCA Civ 312, [2012] 3 All ER 380.
[215] [2010] EWCA Civ 392, [2010] 4 All ER 600.
[216] [2010] EWCA Civ 1282, [2011] 3 All ER 348.

Pages 742-744
Tort liability, compensation and the Human Rights Act

The award of compensation by way of 'just satisfaction' for breach of Convention rights became possible under the Human Rights Act 1998, s 8. But, as explained in the text, this has not led to the making of many successful new claims for compensation in respect of official wrongdoing. In *A v Essex Council*,[217] a severely autistic boy with serious behavioural and communication difficulties had to be withdrawn from a special day school that he was attending. He remained at home for 18 months until he was admitted to a suitable specialist boarding school: during this time the council gave his parents limited help with educational materials. The Supreme Court by a majority held that Article 2 of the First Protocol to the ECHR (the right to education) did not guarantee an absolute right to a minimum standard of education: the delay in arranging for him to attend a suitable school was not a denial of access to the educational system.

Delay of a different kind featured in *R (MK (Iran)) v SSHD*.[218] An Iranian who claimed asylum in September 2004 and was not granted indefinite leave to remain until January 2010 sought damages for the delay, claiming that this had caused or aggravated his mental health problems; he relied both on European regulations stipulating the procedure for dealing with asylum applications (text, pages 339–341) and on his ECHR rights. The Court of Appeal held that (1) the EU regulations did not provide the basis for a claim for damages for unlawful delay, and (2) under Article 6(1) ECHR, asylum claims were not regarded as raising questions of 'civil rights': while the delay in reaching the decision had been so unreasonable as to be unlawful, and had breached the Secretary of State's public law duty to decide the application within a reasonable time, the delay gave rise to no financial remedy, even if it had caused MK to suffer provable loss.

The Court of Appeal's decision in *Anufrijeva v Southwark Council* (text, page 743) was influential in *R (TG) v Lambeth Council*,[219] where the council had acted wrongly in dealing with the claimant under housing legislation (and not under the Children Act 1989) at a time when he was under 18. The court granted judicial review of the council's decision as to TG's current status, but it refused to permit TG to proceed with a claim for compensation based on Article 8 ECHR, holding that the Strasbourg case-law did not in general support such a claim when this arose from a state's failure to provide a home or other financial support for the claimant.

These decisions may be contrasted with that in *TTM v Hackney Council*, noted above in relation to habeas corpus (and see Chapter 31, pages 726–729) where the claim for compensation was founded on the right to liberty at common law; the

---

[217] [2010] UKSC 33, [2011] 1 AC 280. This decision followed one on the right to education made in *Ali v Head Teacher of Lord Grey School* [2006] UKHL 14, [2006] 2 AC 363.

[218] [2010] EWCA Civ 115, [2010] 4 All ER 892.

[219] [2011] EWCA Civ 526, [2011] 4 All ER 453.

parties agreed that (under the Human Rights Act 1998, s 3) the court should 'read down' the Mental Health Act 1983, s 139 to enable the claim to succeed against the local authority. And in *Rabone v Pennine Care NHS Trust*,[220] the Supreme Court awarded compensation under the Human Rights Act 1998, s 8, by way of 'just satisfaction' of a claim by parents for breach of Article 2 ECHR when their daughter, an informal psychiatric patient considered to be at 'moderate to high' risk of suicide, was released from hospital on home leave (against the wishes of her parents) and hanged herself a day later.

Page 744
Other aspects of governmental liability

Two decisions of the Supreme Court regarding the application of the law of restitution to schemes may be noted. In *R (Child Poverty Action Group) v Work and Pensions Secretary*,[221] it was held that the Secretary of State had no power based on the common law of restitution to recover any payments of social security benefit that were found to have been overpaid; the reason for this was that the social security legislation was intended to provide an exclusive scheme for recovering overpayments of benefit, and statutory changes in that scheme had not revived the common law in this area of social provision. The proceedings in *Test Claimants in the Franked Investment Income Group Litigation v Revenue and Customs Commissioners*[222] involved a complex question as to whether legislation by the UK Parliament complied with EU law, and a reference to the European Court of Justice was made. The Supreme Court also restated the principle in *Woolwich Building Society v Inland Revenue Commissioners (No 2)* (text, page 744) where it was disputed whether it applied only when a specific demand from the Revenue to pay tax had been made. On this issue, holding that it was not necessary to show that such a demand had been made, Lord Walker said: 'We should restate the *Woolwich* principle to cover all sums paid to a public authority (and sufficiently causally connected) with an apparent statutory authority to pay tax which (in fact and in law) is not lawfully due.'[223]

Pages 744-746
Tort liability and judicial review

As may be seen from the text, the interaction between the tort liability of public authorities and the effect of judicial review on their acts and decisions often

---

[220] [2012] UKSC 2, [2012] AC 72.
[221] [2010] UKSC 54, [2011] 1 All ER 729.
[222] [2012] UKSC 19, [2012] 3 All ER 909.
[223] Ibid, para [79].

presents difficult situations for the courts. The Supreme Court's decision in *R (Lumba) (Congo)* v *Home Secretary*[224] has been noted in relation to the detention and deportation of foreign nationals after they have completed their prison sentences (see commentary on Chapter 20 B, above). The nine-judge court held unanimously that it was unlawful in public law for the Secretary of State to operate an unpublished policy which was inconsistent with published policy, but the court was divided on the consequences of this. The majority (six judges) held that the actual detention had been unlawful and gave rise to an award of damages. However, three of these judges (Lords Collins, Kerr and Dyson) held that, since the detainees would have been lawfully detained anyway, they had suffered no loss and should recover only nominal damages of £1 each. The other three of the majority judges (Lord Hope, Lord Walker and Lady Hale) held that damages should be awarded of a 'conventional' amount that would reflect the importance of the right of liberty and the seriousness of the infringement (payments of £500 or £1000 to each claimant were suggested). A minority of three judges (Lords Phillips, Brown and Rodger) held that, because the claimants would have been lawfully detained in any event, there was no liability for false imprisonment. The judgments in this case included wide-ranging discussion of the principles of public law that applied and of the various forms of damages that are available (nominal, vindictive, exemplary, conventional etc).

In a case concerning similar facts, *R (Kambadzi)* v *Home Secretary*[225], the Home Office failed to conduct regular reviews of the detention pending deportation of a Zimbabwean, who had completed a prison sentence for serious offences; the Home Office's published policy required regular review and said that 'to be lawful', detention must conform with the stated policy. By 3-2, the Supreme Court held that the executive's failure to adhere to its published policy without good reason amounted to an abuse of power that rendered the detention itself unlawful.

As stated earlier in comments on Chapter 29 D (The Parliamentary Ombudsman), the poor reception given to the Law Commission's paper, *Administrative Redress: Public Bodies and the Citizen*, led to the Commission's decision in 2010 to abandon proposals for a widespread reform of the liability of public authorities, including the question of compensation in connection with judicial review.

Pages 755-760
Public interest immunity

The brief account (text, pages 759–760) of the current operation of public interest immunity (PII) includes an account of the remarkable proceedings in *R (Binyam Mohamed)* v *Foreign Secretary*[226] in which the Court of Appeal robustly insisted on

---

[224] [2011] UKSC 12, [2012] 1 AC 245.
[225] [2011] UKSC 23, [2011] 4 All ER 975.
[226] [2010] EWCA Civ 65, [2010] 4 All ER 91.

including in its judgment seven brief paragraphs which the Foreign Secretary had argued would prejudice co-operation between the British and American security services. The nature of the balancing exercise that was undertaken by the court is summarised in *R (Binyam Mohamed) v Foreign Secretary (No 2)*:[227] among the relevant factors was that 'there is nothing inherently sensitive in the information in those paragraphs'.[228] These decisions were made in the course of a complex history of litigation brought by former detainees at Guantanamo Bay in which they sought damages from the UK government for illegal acts that they claimed occurred when they were detained, and during their rendition (text, page 446), interrogation and detention in American custody. To resist these claims, and arguing that it was impractical to go through the PII process, the government urged the court to order a 'closed material procedure' by which sensitive security material in its possession could be made known to special advocates, appointed to act for the claimants, so that part of the defence case would not be revealed to the claimants or to their lawyers. As stated in the text (page 760, note 254), Silber J held that the court had power to order a closed material procedure on a civil claim for damages, despite the absence of any statutory authority for this. That decision was reversed by the Court of Appeal, after which these claims for damages were settled on confidential terms.[229] The central issue of principle nonetheless came to the Supreme Court. In *Al Rawi v Security Service*,[230] nine judges were unanimous that the courts have no power simply to replace the normal process of PII with a closed material procedure. A majority of six judges further held that after the PII process has been completed, the court has no power at common law to introduce a closed material procedure, appointing special advocates and so on, since this would be a radical departure from the principles of open and natural justice, and would deny parties their common law right to a fair trial. In the majority view, existing exceptions to the principle that justice must be done in open court (for instance, to protect the interests of a child or in intellectual property law to keep secret a commercial interest) did not justify introducing a controversial new rule in all civil litigation. Such a fundamental change in civil procedure, if it were to be made, must be made by Parliament. A minority of three judges (Lord Mance, Lord Clarke and Lady Hale) were less categorical than the majority, holding that in some circumstances the court may have power to order a closed material procedure where difficulties remain after the PII process has been completed.

Alongside *Al Rawi*, the Supreme Court also decided *Home Office v Tariq*.[231] The Employment Tribunals Act 1996 authorises the Secretary of State to make regulations authorising employment tribunals to adopt a closed material procedure if the

---

[227] [2010] EWCA Civ 158, [2010] 4 All ER 177.

[228] *Al Rawi and others v Security Service* [2010] EWCA Civ 65, [2010] 4 All ER 91, para [170] (Lord Neuberger MR).

[229] [2010] EWCA Civ 482.

[230] [2011] UKSC 34, [2012] 1 AC 531.

[231] [2011] UKSC 35, [2012] 1 AC 452. And see text, page 564.

interests of national security so require. Tariq, an immigration officer who had been suspended on security grounds, challenged an order applying closed material procedure to his claim against the Home Office for discrimination on grounds of race and religion, relying on the ECHR and on EU law. By 8-1, the Supreme Court upheld the closed material procedure in employment cases, holding that the system contains sufficient safeguards to protect the claimant's interests. In dissent, Lord Kerr held that withholding of information from a claimant is a breach of the common law right to a fair trial, and also a breach of the right to a fair trial under Article 6(1) ECHR.[232]

The Supreme Court's decision in *Al Rawi* that the courts had no power to introduce a closed material procedure in civil proceedings caused the government to introduce legislation to give the courts that novel power.[233] The resulting Bill met very strong criticism, particularly in the House of Lords[234], and some limitations on the government's original proposals were adopted. Part 2 of the Justice and Security Act 2013 authorises the High Court, Court of Session and higher courts in the course of civil proceedings to decide (on the application of the Secretary of State, any party to the proceedings, or of its own motion) that 'closed material procedure' (CMP) may be followed. Such procedure applies where 'sensitive material' (defined as 'material the disclosure of which would be damaging to the interests of national security', s 6(11)) would otherwise require to be disclosed (or withheld) by the party in question and where 'it is in the interests of the fair and effective administration of justice' that the procedure should apply (s 6(5)). Before applying to the court, the Secretary of State must have considered whether a claim for public interest immunity (PII) should be made (s 6(7)). The decision of the court authorising CMP must be kept under review by the court and may be revoked if the 'fair and effective administration of justice' no longer requires it (s 7(3)). Before the court authorises CMP, a 'special advocate' must be appointed by a law officer of the Crown to represent the interests of the party adversely affected by the CMP (s 9(1)): the litigant and his or her regular legal representatives cannot be informed of the material in question. When CMP is authorised by the court, proceedings involving the sensitive material take place in strict secrecy but in the presence of the special advocate; the eventual judgment of the court will require to be in two parts, one an open judgment covering matters dealt with in open court, and the other a secret judgment that cannot be published or disclosed to the litigant, and can be seen only by the Secretary of State and the special advocates. The Act authorises rules of court to be made to give effect to CMP. It requires the Secretary of State to report to Parliament

---

[232] Lord Kerr considered to be anomalous the decision of the Strasbourg Court in *Kennedy* v *UK* (18 May 2010) which, in a case of suspected telephone tapping brought under the Regulation of Investigatory Powers Act 2000 (text, pages 481–6), held that Kennedy had no absolute right to see all relevant evidence and that the UK legislation did not breach Articles 6(1) and 8 ECHR.

[233] See the Green Paper, *Justice and Security* (Cm 8194, 2011); and observations by the Joint Committee on Human Rights (24th report, HL paper 286, HC 1777, 2010–12).

[234] House of Lords Constitution Committee, *Justice and Security Bill* (3rd report, HL Paper 18, 2012–13).

each year on the use made of CMP (s 12); and after five years a review of the operation of Part 2 of the Act must be commissioned by the Secretary of State and laid in Parliament (s 13). It remains to be seen whether the structure for decision-making contained in the Act will enable the courts to make decisions independently of the executive on matters that may have a bearing on national security, but may also (as with rendition and prolonged detention in Guantanamo Bay) have a drastic effect on the individual's rights and liberties and on the due process of law.